Window Boxes and Terraces

TORSTAR BOOKS
NEW YORK · TORONTO

Torstar Books Inc, 41 Madison Avenue, Suite 2900, New York, NY 10010 in collaboration with ICA-förlaget AB, Västerås, Sweden.

Library of Congress Cataloging in Publication Data
Window boxes and terraces.
   (Living with houseplants)
   Includes index.
   1. Container gardening.   2. Window-gardening.
I. Torstar Books (Firm)   II. Series.
SB418.W56   1986   635.9'86   86–19235

ISBN 1–55001–064–6 (Living With Houseplants Series)
ISBN 1–55001–066–2 (Window Boxes and Terraces)

10 9 8 7 6 5 4 3 2 1
Printed in Belgium

CONTENTS

Introduction	4
Window boxes	6
Making and securing	8
Planting	10
Seasonal suggestions	12
Hanging baskets	14
Watering and planting	16
Balconies	17
Terraces and patios	22
Container plants: basic care	29
Containers	30
Houseplants outdoors	34
African blue lily (*Agapanthus africanus*)	35
Agave (*Agave americana*)	36
Love-lies-bleeding (*Amaranthus caudatus*)	37
Bellflower (*Campanula poscharskyana*)	38
Lantana (*Lantana camara*)	39
Flowering annuals	40
Snapdragon (*Antirrhinum majus*)	42
China aster (*Callistephus chinensis*)	43
Cathedral bell (*Cobaea scandens*)	44
Dahlia (*Dahlia* × *cultorum*)	46
Cape marigold (*Dimorphotheca sinuata*)	47
California poppy (*Eschscholzia californica*)	48
Candytuft (*Iberis umbellata*)	49
Morning glory (*Ipomoea tricolor*)	50
Herb tree-mallow (*Lavatera trimestris*)	51
Monkey flower (*Mimulus luteus*)	52
Nemesia (*Nemesia strumosa*)	53
Flowering tobacco (*Nicotiana alata*)	54
Geranium (*Pelargonium* × *hortorum*)	55
Penstemon (*Penstemon* × *gloxinioides*)	56
Petunia (*Petunia* × *hybrida*)	57
Harebell phacelia (*Phacelia campanularia*)	58
Sage (*Salvia*)	59
Butterfly flower (*Schizanthus* × *wisetonensis*)	60
Dusty miller (*Senecio cineraria*)	61
Black-eyed Susan (*Thunbergia alata*)	62
Zinnia (*Zinnia elegans*)	63
Trees and shrubs	64
Climbing plants	66
Water gardens	67
Herbs, vegetables and fruit	68
Index	70
Acknowledgments	72

Introduction

Container gardening is as much fun as it is rewarding. To spend a summer's evening sitting out on your patio or terrace, surrounded by the fruits of your labor – colorful flowers, sweet-scented shrubs, delicate aromatic herbs, perhaps under the shade of a leafy vine or clematis – this is simple pleasure indeed.

To decorate walls with hanging baskets and window ledges with flower boxes is not only a joy to you but also to your neighbors and passers-by. Even if the space available is restricted, you can still transform a small area into an attractive feature with flowers in containers. For many city dwellers, this may be the only form of outdoor gardening possible. A concrete backyard, a dull flight of steps, a flat roof, a narrow balcony several floors up – all these areas can be enlivened with a little work, some expense and a lot of imagination. If you do not have the horizontal space, you can always use the vertical, with hanging baskets, wall containers, trellis work, pergolas and tall plant stands carrying several pots.

There are many advantages to growing plants in containers. It is not hard work like digging the garden, young and old can do it and you do not need a "green thumb" for success. Containers can easily be moved to take advantage of changing light or temperature conditions, to make room if you are having a party, to change the color scheme in a particular area, or simply removed when the flowers are past their best.

Since plants are, by definition, contained in containers, more care must be taken over their watering and feeding needs. The plants cannot reach out with their roots in search of moisture or nutrients as they can in garden soil. You have to provide both. There are many proprietary potting mixes available. Some are soil-based, others soilless in which case you need to fertilize after about 6 weeks. During flowering, feed your plants about once every 2 weeks as a general rule. Never allow the soil to dry out in a container. Use your finger to test for moisture content. Drainage is vital; most containers have holes in the bottom, but if they do not, drill them yourself. Before planting, place clay shards over the holes, followed by a layer of leaf mold or peat to aid drainage, and then a suitable potting mix.

There are a great variety of containers to choose from, made in all shapes and sizes from various materials – plastic, terracotta, fiberglass, metal, wood, reconstituted stone. Your choice should be influenced by the practicality and durability of the containers, as well as the color, form and texture of your plants and the surroundings in which you place them. The plainest containers often work best since they do not distract from the plants. On the other hand, a classic terracotta or stone pedestal urn can become the focal point on a patio and might be planted with a simple one-color scheme so as not to detract from its lines.

Vegetables can also be grown in containers and it is possible to be extremely productive even in a small area. Lettuces and radishes, for instance, can be grown in window boxes, tomatoes in growing bags, strawberries in wooden barrels, peas or beans trained up bamboo poles in tubs, or zuccini in troughs or sinks. Besides providing you with fresh

LIMITS OF AVERAGE ANNUAL MINIMUM TEMPERATURES FOR HARDINESS ZONES

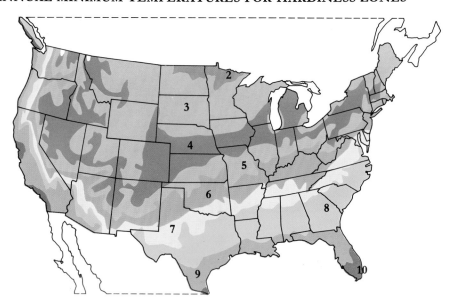

2	−50°F to −35°F
3	−35°F to −20°F
4	−20°F to −10°F
5	−10°F to −5°F
6	−5°F to 5°F
7	5°F to 10°F
8	10°F to 20°F
9	20°F to 30°F
10	30°F to 40°F

food, some vegetables also have lovely flowers – the purple heads of chives, the yellow flowers of tomatoes and squashes, or the sweet-pea type flowers of peas and beans.

There is an endless variety of plants with which to stock your containers. There are bedding annuals, perennials, climbers, trailers, small shrubs, ornamental trees, dwarf conifers and a whole range of flowers grown from bulbs, corms and tubers to give interest throughout the year. Stunning displays can be made from color varieties of the same plant; the balcony (*above*) with its overhanging window boxes is transformed into an exotic place by its collection of busy lizzies.

How hardy are plants?

Whether a plant will survive in a particular climate is determined by the lowest temperature it will have to endure. A useful, though generalized, indicator is given in the "Hardiness Zones" map opposite. This shows the country divided into 9 zones, based on average annual minimum temperatures, ranging from $-50°F$ to $40°F$. These zones were defined in 1938 by Harvard University's Arnold Arboretum and are still broadly used by growers to describe the hardiness of plants. For example, to say that gardenia is "hardy to Zone 8" means that it will not tolerate temperatures below $10°F$ (i.e. generally speaking, it will not grow in Zones 2–7).

5

Window boxes

One of the great joys of window boxes is the variety of pleasures they provide. A colorful display of flowers outside the windows not only cheers up the interior of your house or apartment, it also transforms the exterior. Passers-by will get pleasure from your display, as will neighbors who may suddenly be motivated to brighten up their own ledges.

Nor is the window-box gardener restricted to growing flowering plants. Enormous satisfaction can be derived from growing fresh vegetables and herbs just outside your window. Lettuces, radishes, dwarf varieties of tomatoes and low-growing herbs will provide an attractive, handy harvest.

Before installing a window box, check with your local town or city buildings department if there are any regulations governing siting and fixing. Satisfy yourself that the position you have in mind is indeed safe. Structural deterioration – rotting wood, crumbling stonework, missing mortar between bricks – may reach quite an advanced state before it becomes glaringly obvious. Close inspection at this early stage is clearly essential. Do not install boxes until any defects have been remedied. It is your responsibility to make sure that faulty installation does not lead to a serious, possibly fatal, accident.

Other factors governing siting will include the position of the window – plants will not thrive unless they get a lot of sunshine; dappled shade is the most they will tolerate – the way the window opens and, of course, whether or not you have a window ledge. Sash windows or casement windows that open inwards pose no problems for ledge siting; where windows open outward or there is no ledge at all the box will have to be supported on the wall just below the window. In both cases, the box must be absolutely securely retained with extra-strong brackets; instructions on ways of achieving this are given on page 8.

Once the box has been firmly anchored in position, you can begin to prepare it for planting (see p. 10 for details). Do not attempt to do this before positioning, since once planted it will be almost impossible to maneuver.

An alternative to semi-permanent planting is to fill the box with several plants still contained in their individual pots. The advantage of this is that it enables you to change your display with the minimum fuss; if the pots are plunged up to their

Matching window boxes (*below*), brimming over with bright geraniums, make a good display all through the summer months. When colder weather sets in, boxes can still be interesting (*right*) with, for example, a planting of trailing evergreen ivy (*Hedera*), asparagus fern (*Asparagus densiflorus*), flanked by variegated *Euonymus*, and Jerusalem cherry (*Solanum pseudocapsicum*), with its cheerful winter berries ranging in color from green to bright orange.

rims in moist peat (as it done for double potting indoor plants) moisture loss will be slower.

Remember that tall plants are not really suitable for window boxes. They will not withstand the winds to which they will be exposed from time to time. Exceptions to this rule are the popular dwarf conifers; these sturdy subjects could be part of a permanent window-box planting, acting as a backdrop to the more colorful seasonal flowering plants. Suggestions for achieving a year-round display are given on page 12 while the cultivation of a wide range of annual flowering plants is discussed on pages 40–63. Whatever plants you choose, taller specimens should go at the side of the box if you want to see out of the window.

Window boxes are obtainable in a variety of colors and materials. Though the lighter plastic or fiberglass kinds are a sensible choice in many ways, they may not offer the best choice of color. Dark or muted colors are preferable; white will not wear well if the air is even slightly polluted and might stand out too much against the background. Try to choose a color that blends in with the color of the window frame. Wood, as long as it has been treated with a safe preservative, is probably the most attractive material. It is not too difficult to make your own wooden box, if you have some basic carpentry skills: you will find a guide to constructing a simple box on page 8. As a general rule it should not be more than 3 feet in length.

Making and securing window boxes

It is really quite simple to make a wooden window box. If you can afford it, redwood is the best choice since it looks good and does not need treating with preservative. Hardwoods, such as oak, elm or teak, last much longer than softwoods such as pine, although pressure-treated pine will last for years.

The wood should be $\frac{3}{4}$–1 inch thick. Cut the planks to size – the optimum easily portable length is 3 feet. The box should be at least 9 inches deep and 9 inches across, to allow adequate depth for root development and enough space for planting. Good drainage is very important and 1-inch holes should be drilled at 1-foot intervals in the center of the base plank. It is a good idea to insert plastic drainage plugs in the holes to protect the wood from rotting. Reinforcing corner battens, cut to the height of the box, are very important since they strengthen the whole structure. Glue them on to the insides of the end pieces and then assemble the whole box, through the battens, with zinc-coated screws, which do not rust. The diagram *(top)* shows you how.

Securing window boxes
It is vital for safety that window boxes are made secure at any level above the ground floor. You can fix two strong metal brackets to the wall on either side, as well as chain supports if necessary. If the ledge is uneven or slopes downward, screw three tapered wedges to the base so that the box is kept level. A metal guard rail screwed into the side walls, and further secured to the outer window frame (if this does not interfere with the opening of the window), will also help to retain the box. On a long ledge where you may have two boxes or more, it is advisable to reinforce the guard rail against strong winds with brackets attached at intervals to the ledge *(see bottom diagram)*. If you have no window ledge, attach the box directly to the wall with the support of strong metal brackets beneath.

CONSTRUCTION

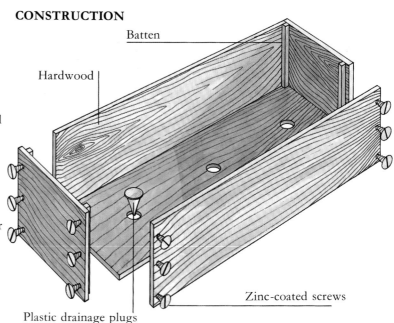

Batten

Hardwood

Zinc-coated screws

Plastic drainage plugs

BRACKETS

WEDGES

DOUBLE WINDOW BOXES

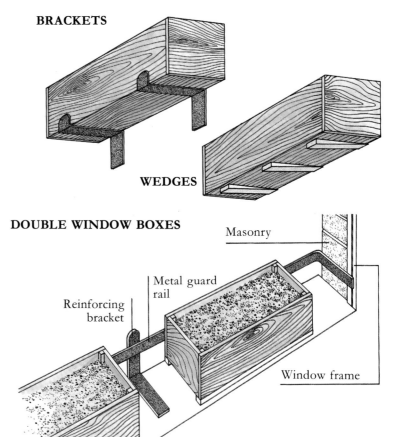

Masonry

Metal guard rail

Reinforcing bracket

Window frame

An all-white display is dazzling against the dark
background. The window box is effectively hidden
by the luxuriant growth of carefully chosen plants.
They complement each other in color, yet contrast in
terms of leaf texture and flower form – tall
geraniums, fluffy petunias, neat begonias, busy lizzies
and trailing lobelias. Similar displays can be made in
red with salvias, zinnias and fuchsias.

Planting window boxes

Having treated your window box with a safe timber preservative inside and several coats of varnish or paint outside, you are now ready to plant up. Put the box in its final position, remembering about safety and security. First, add the drainage layer over the holes – pieces of clay shards, brick, small stones or a layer of gravel. To assist drainage, you can screw two wooden battens along the base of the box to lift it off the ledge. Fit a plastic drip tray beneath to catch excess water.

Follow the drainage layer with 1 inch of peat, leaf mold or a piece of lawn turf with the grass-side down. This layer helps to retain moisture at root level in very hot weather. Fill the box to within 1 inch of its rim with a standard potting mix. Firm the soil down and water it thoroughly. Now you are ready to put in your plants – ranging from dwarf conifers to trailing ivies and flowering annuals.

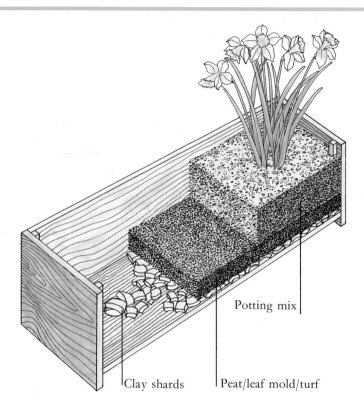

Potting mix

Clay shards | Peat/leaf mold/turf

Occasional showers of rain in summer will refresh your window boxes. But do remember the ones where rain cannot reach – those that may be sheltered under an overhanging eave or ledge.

Cacti are unusual candidates for a window box but in a sunny warm position, they do very well. Leave the plants in their individual pots and spread bark mulch or pea gravel over the surface to help retain moisture. Cacti can be left outdoors through the fall and even into the first frosts, but then bring them indoors for winter. Note the metal guard rail to keep this box safe on its high window ledge.

BULBS AND CORMS

Many beautiful flowers, ideally suited to container gardening, grow from bulbs and corms. Daffodils, tulips, crocuses and hyacinths are all familiar springtime plants of this kind. But there are many more you can grow at other times to give year-round color, including autumn crocuses, winter aconites, gladioli, cyclamens, lilies of the valley, fritillarias, lilies and irises.

In a bulb or corm, the roots grow from the flattened plate at the base (which is actually the reduced stem), so this part must always be planted downward in the soil. When you buy bulbs, there may be tiny roots already growing which will show you the correct orientation. Sometimes the bud may have started to sprout and this, of course, gives another clue – green parts always grow up toward the light.

The second point about planting bulbs is how deep to place them in the soil. As a general rule, the base of the bulb should be planted at a depth equal to $2\frac{1}{2}$ to 3 times its greatest diameter. There are, as always, exceptions to the rule. For example, the bulb of *Lilium candidum*, despite its robust size, must be planted at only about 2 inches below the surface, while nerine lilies like their tops protruding out of the soil.

A good standard potting mix is suitable for filling bulb containers. But you must make sure that the soil is well-drained. Bulbs in waterlogged conditions will rot. You may, therefore need to lighten your soil by mixing in some organic matter (peat or leaf mold) or sand.

To plant a bulb, dig out a U-shaped hole in the soil at the required depth, put a little bone meal or superphosphate (which encourages root development) into the hole and push the bulb gently down. By planting a variety of bulbs at different levels in a tub or window box, you can achieve a continuous display of many colors, shapes and heights.

After flowering, cut out the flower stems but leave the foliage. This is essential since the plant needs to continue making food to store in the bulb for next year's growth. Continue watering and feeding for about 6 weeks or until the leaves die down and turn yellow. Then remove the bulbs, clean loose soil off and store them in a cool dark place until planting out again. If you have the space, let the leaves die down undisturbed in their original container. If you need the container for other plants, transplant the bulbs into the garden or into another container.

Seasonal suggestions for window boxes

SPRINGTIME

Bulbs, planted in the previous year's fall, provide the main display at this time of year. No spring window box is complete without bulbs of daffodils (**1**) and tulips (**2**); a lower tier of hyacinths (**3**) and grape hyacinths (**4**), with crocuses (**5**) beneath. Primroses (**6**) and dwarf wallflowers (**7**) add their own fragrances; pinch out the growing tips of wallflowers to make them bushier. Trailing ivy (**8**) disguises the front edge of the box. You may like a multicolored scheme or a harmonizing theme of, for example, yellow and blue. Whatever you prefer, the choice is there, with endless color varieties available.

SUMMERTIME

Luxuriant growth and warm colors burst from a typical summer window box where zonal geraniums (**1**), with their striking leaves and flowers, jostle with daisylike marguerites (**2**) in the back row. Pansies (**3**) and petunias (**4**) are great favorites, with many color varieties. Fluffy blue *Ageratum* (**5**), with heads like shaving brushes, also comes in pink or white. Trailing lobelia (**6**) and a variegated ivy (**7**), such as *Hedera helix* 'Jubilee' or 'Goldenheart,' add the finishing touches around the edges. Other suggestions include marigolds, alyssum, nasturtiums, verbena, stock, fuchsias and salvias.

WINTERTIME

There are many hardy evergreen plants that will grow happily outdoors so long as the position is not too cold or exposed. In a mild climate an effective display might be a group of heathers (**1**), dwarf conifers (**2**), evergreen ivy (**3**) and foliage plants such as the dusty miller, *Senecio* (**4**). There are many varieties of the hardy heather *Erica carnea* which will flower in the depths of winter. Dwarf conifers like the golden *Chamaecyparis* or the blue-green *Juniperus* do well in boxes. Other plants might include saxifragas, sedums and dwarf cotoneasters, with the bonus of red winter berries.

All-time favorites for window boxes, hanging baskets, tubs, in fact any container, are geraniums and lobelia. There are numerous varieties of both available, in various colors and growth habits. This ivy-leaved 'geranium' (*Pelargonium peltatum*) and the trailing lobelia flower profusely from early to late summer. You can induce more flowering by dead-heading the plants when necessary.

Hanging baskets

Lush cascades of trailing flowers have been popular since ancient times: the Hanging Gardens of Babylon were one of the wonders of the ancient world. Nowadays, hanging baskets are used both in and outside the house and their cheerful display enhances the facades of shops and public buildings as well as sidewalks. The same welcoming and friendly atmosphere can be achieved at home on patio, porch, deck and terrace.

Hanging baskets and wall-mounted containers come in a variety of shapes and sizes. The traditional "old-fashioned" wire basket is still often the best choice since it increases the planting possibilities. Insure that the mesh is large enough to make planting through the sides fairly easy. Hanging pots made from cellulose fiber may only last for two years, but they hold a good volume of potting soil and do not dry out as rapidly as wire baskets.

A number of other hanging containers are available, many made of plastic which may be in a mesh or solid form. Often, a clip-on drip tray is provided for catching excess water, an especially good feature if the basket is hanging in a porch or roofed patio area where unsightly puddles will not evaporate away so quickly as outdoors. Generally, the plastic containers are not very beautiful, and it may never be possible to disguise those that only allow top planting.

Hanging pots, which are primarily intended for houseplants, can also be used outdoors. However, their possibilities are limited and they are not a substitute for proper hanging baskets. Some hanging pots have large holes around the rim and offer greater scope for planting trailing flowers.

Collapsible baskets, of the kind originally intended for the kitchen, come in one, two or even three tiers. They can be filled with a collection of various flowers to produce a stunning effect. However, the combined weight of soil, water and plants in three baskets can be considerable, so make sure that they are firmly supported by extra-strong chains and brackets. The same precaution should be taken with all types of hanging container. The brackets used should be strong and big enough to hold the planted basket and its contents clear of the walls.

Choose the location for your hanging containers carefully. Positioned too high and they will be difficult to tend, too low and they will constantly be in the way. Avoid a position which receives constant wind since this dries out the soil even more than sunshine. The use of a swivel-arm wall bracket means that the basket can be swung around during the day so that all the plants receive an equal share of light. Another important consideration is watering. Since this may be necessary once or even twice a day in the height of summer, containers should be easily accessible.

HANGING CONTAINERS

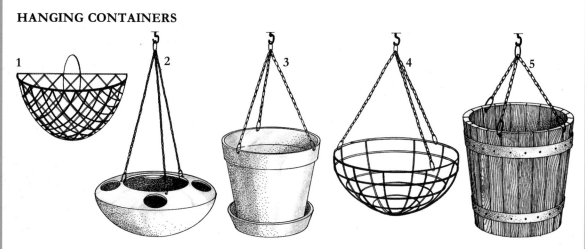

There is a great variety of hanging containers available, but a selection might include a wall-mounted basket made of plastic-covered wire (**1**); plastic hanging pot with holes for planting trailers (**2**); plastic pot with built-in drip tray (**3**) suspended on plastic wires; traditional wire basket (**4**), hung on chains, probably the most versatile for top and side planting, and available in various diameters, from 9 to 15 inches; wooden barrel (**5**), suspended on chains looks well in a "rural" setting, but the timber must be treated regularly, and weight may be a problem.

Almost any type of container, ranging from a copper
tea kettle, with holes bored in the base, to a dog's
wicker basket, can be made into a hanging "basket."
Here a more conventional plastic pot, with a built-in
drip tray, is suspended on chains and is planted with
a beautiful trailing geranium.

Planting and watering hanging baskets

PLANTING

WATERING

When planting the traditional wire-mesh hanging basket steady it first on an empty bucket. Put a thick layer of sphagnum moss in the bottom, followed by a couple of handfuls of potting mix. Push a few small trailing plants (such as lobelia) roots first through the openings in the mesh and firm them down in the soil. Build up a 1-inch-thick lining of moss around the sides of the basket and continue the moss, potting mix, planting sequence until you reach the top, where the larger bushy plants are added.

If you only have a watering can and a stepladder or high stool at your disposal, watering your luxuriantly growing baskets or wall-mounted containers may prove so arduous that you will be tempted to neglect them. Hosepipe attachments for reaching up are available, but it is much cheaper and just as effective to improvise your own. Simply take an appropriate length of bamboo pole or garden cane and lash the hosepipe to it with twine or even rubber bands. Attach a sprinkler rose for a gentle shower.

The rewards of regular watering and lots of sunshine are profuse blooms.

Balconies

A balcony, brightened by a collection of colorful blooms and perhaps a few vegetable plants, will be a constant source of pleasure to its owner. Nor need balcony gardening be considered simply a summertime activity: even during the winter months, an assortment of evergreen plants will provide continuing interest, enlivening what might otherwise be a rather dismal prospect.

Balcony gardeners have a distinct advantage over those who are restricted to window boxes, namely floor space. Apart from providing more growing room, the floor allows greater freedom of movement to tend your plants.

Before embarking on any ambitious plans for balcony gardens, it is obviously essential that weight should be taken into consideration. Choose lightweight containers and remember that the main contribution to weight will be watered soil. An average size trough will absorb 2 gallons of water (weighing some 20 pounds). This, plus the weight of the soil and the plants, could immediately produce a total weight of about 56 pounds for a single trough. It is, therefore, essential to make sure

that a balcony is strong enough to support a considerable weight before you load it, otherwise the consequences will be disastrous. Take expert advice if in doubt.

Balcony gardeners must also be aware of neighbors below as well as pedestrians on the sidewalk, particularly when watering. Some balconies have an integral drainage system which will take care of over-enthusiastic watering, but if such a system does not exist, the provision of adequate drip trays under containers will take care of excess water.

Since many balconies are situated well above ground level, they are often subject to strong buffeting by the wind. This not only affects your choice of plants, restricting you, for instance, to low-growing or strong-stemmed types, it may also mean that fallen leaves, and even soil (in dry weather), may be blown onto or even into neighboring apartments. Keep the area meticulously tidy and swept every day. This attention means neighbors are less likely to be upset and also prevents unwanted bugs or insects breeding in heaps of leaves or soil.

Above: All possible growing space has been utilized on this balcony. Besides containers on the floor, there are troughs at a higher level, a hanging basket and a trellis, fixed between the outer walls, all of which provide growing space.

The balcony gardener does not need a wide range of tools (*right*). You can manage perfectly adequately with little more than a household knife and spoon. However, maintenance tasks can be carried out more easily and efficiently with the proper tools. Those shown here, plus a watering can, will fulfill most needs. Pruning shears or secateurs (**1**); two trowels, one with a rounded tip (**2**) for top dressing and planting, the other (**3**) with a pointed end for seedlings and small plants; a weeding knife (**4**) with a hollow blade for weeding in confined spaces; a handfork (**5**) for weeding and loosening the soil; a 3- or 5½-pint sprayer (**6**) for misting (use another sprayer if you have to treat plants with insecticide). Not shown, but absolutely vital, is a watering can with a long spout or, if there are a lot of plants, a length of hose.

TOOLS FOR BALCONY GARDENING

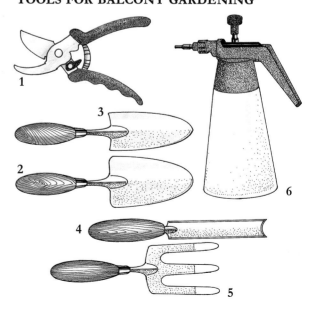

GROWING BAGS

Plastic growing bags are excellent for small-scale gardening. They come in various sizes and are filled with a specially formulated, peat-based growing medium. They are clean, easy to use, economic and lightweight.

Apart from flowers, you can produce a great crop of shallow-rooting vegetables from growing bags, such as lettuces, tomatoes, peppers, zuccini and eggplants.

Position the growing bag in a sunny sheltered spot. Follow the manufacturer's instructions for planting; you can make a few slits in the base of the bag for drainage. Special frames can be purchased and, with bamboo canes slotted between, will provide support for vegetables such as tomatoes.

Balcony gardeners are not necessarily restricted to conventional containers. With some flair and imagination, other things can be used to produce highly attractive displays. Here, a two-tone scheme of geraniums has been planted in, among other things, some plastic pails. When improvising containers, always ensure that there is adequate drainage. Pierce holes in the bottom if possible and include a substantial layer of drainage shards before adding your potting mix.

Containers for balconies

Choosing the right kind of container for your balcony is important, but do not overlook the potential dangers of excessive weight. Timber, when treated with a safe preservative, is an obvious choice since it can be painted or varnished to complement the surrounding color scheme. Containers made of plastic or fiberglass have advantages because they are relatively lightweight and soil in them will dry out less quickly than that in wooden containers. To create an overall feeling of uniformity, while still maintaining interest, use containers made of the same material but of different shapes and sizes. If your balcony can support their weight, containers made from terracotta are probably unbeatable, certainly from the visual point of view.

Balcony walls or railings may further increase the available growing space. Evergreen clematis or honeysuckle are vigorous growers and look wonderful tumbling over the railings of a balcony. Train climbing beans up walls and enjoy the culinary as well as the aesthetic results. If walls are strong and wide, window boxes can be secured along them and used to grow both upright and trailing plants. Alternatively, if you do not like the view from the balcony, increase the wall height by fixing a trellis for climbing plants. Tall, wind-resistant plants will not only provide a screen (which will help overcome problems with the view), but will also protect smaller plants on the balcony.

Besides personal preferences, your choice of plants for a balcony will be influenced by the climatic zone of your home's location and the direction in which the balcony faces. This last aspect is vital, since it affects the amount of sunshine and shade to which your plants will be exposed during the course of the day. West-facing balconies, for example, will be subjected to several hours of hot sun during later summer afternoons. Hence, sun-loving plants will thrive while shade lovers should be afforded some protection from the sun's heat.

Obvious flowers to adorn your balcony are upright and trailing geraniums, hanging ivies and lobelia, petunias and fuchsias. There is a huge range of annuals to choose from, a selection of which is shown from page 34 onward.

A low planting of flowers along the edge of a balcony provides a pleasing foreground to the panoramic view beyond. Petunias, with their rich velvety petals and their dark-green leaves, flower profusely during the summer months and are excellent plants for a sunny balcony.

Terraces & patios

A terrace or patio forms an important link between your home and your garden. Whether it be a small backyard or a formal paved area outside your house, you can convert this space into a charming and inviting outdoor "living room," planted with colorful annuals, scented shrubs and even miniature trees. In this extension to your home, you can enjoy meals *al fresco*, entertain your friends to drinks and barbecue suppers, or simply sit quietly and think about all the garden chores that need doing.

Today, we tend to use the words "terrace" and "patio" interchangeably. But, technically, a patio is a courtyard enclosed by four walls and open to the sky. The Moors of North Africa brought the idea of the patio to Europe, developing it first in Spain. This inner courtyard was an area of great family activity, cool and secluded, usually with a central fountain, balconies running around the upper stories and plenty of trees, vines and potted plants giving shade, beauty and tranquillity to this indoor/outdoor garden.

The modern terrace or patio need not be on a grand scale nor be expensive to develop. All you need is a flat dry area sheltered from the winds, preferably near the house for convenience. However, a sunny south- or west-facing corner of the garden may prove a more suitable site in which to build a free-standing terrace or patio, perhaps under the shade of a tree.

Existing walls may provide shelter or you can put up trellis or wattle fencing, all of which provide welcome surfaces for climbers such as *Hydrangea petiolaris*, variegated ivies or honeysuckle. A small enclosed area can be made to look larger by painting the walls white, which has the additional advantage of reflecting more light into the area. A wooden pergola can be built over part of the patio, maybe adjoining the house, to give shade or a little shelter in case of showers. Fast-growing climbers, such as clematis or Virginia creeper, can be trained around the uprights eventually to form a "roof"; in really sunny spots, a grape vine gives the bonus of its fruit.

There is a wide variety of flooring materials for terraces or patios. For cheapness and availability, precast concrete slabs are easy to lay and come in all kinds of color, size and shape. Stone paving is natural-looking in any setting and is available in various textures, ranging from coarse granite through finer sandstone and shale to smooth slate. Wooden decking also looks natural, as do bricks. You can mix materials to great effect, making your patio of, for example, bricks and concrete, decking and cobblestones, or stone and gravel.

Varying the levels of the patio is very effective,

Classic garden design – a wide gravelled terrace leads down a flight of steps, flanked by matching terracotta urns brimming with *Chrysanthemum frutescens*, into the garden proper of rosebeds, lawns, water and mature trees. Such a layout can be scaled down and reproduced for a smaller garden.

even in a small area. Steps can lead down to a sunken area, furnished with garden chairs and table with, perhaps, a small fountain in a pool. The soothing effect of running water and the beauty of such plants as water lilies and sweet flag opens up a whole new dimension for your patio. Paving slabs can be removed here and there to provide deeper soil for a small tree or shrub. Crevices between bricks can be planted with shallow-rooting plants such as campanula or aubretia.

Raised beds, built around the edges of the patio from cement blocks or bricks, are easy to maintain and provide a good depth of soil for shrubs and small trees. These will also provide shade for other plants, which is important, especially if your patio faces west and gets the full strength of the late afternoon sun.

Plants in pots are an integral part of your patio design. They can be easily moved, to catch more shade or sunlight as the day proceeds, or rearranged to give a harmonizing or contrasting color scheme. They can be put aside to make more room if you are having a party or simply taken away when the flowers are past their best. All types of containers can be used: traditional terracotta or modern plastic pots, fiberglass troughs, wooden tubs, strawberry barrels, or unusual containers such as coal scuttles or chimney pots. An old wheelbarrow or even a wooden shoe or rubber boot planted with trailing flowers like nasturtiums or lobelia can look wonderful. Allow your personality to show in this informal relaxing area of the home.

Choose the shape and color of your plants so

THE FORMAL PATIO GARDEN

Good planning and design can transform a small area into a delightful outdoor sitting room, where family and friends can eat and drink in relaxed private surroundings. This small terraced garden has an old-world "Mediterranean" feel, achieved by a careful choice of garden furniture, ornamental containers, mixed paving materials, lighting arrangements and, of course, the plants themselves. Different levels create a feeling of spaciousness and colorful flowers make for a lively show.

The natural stone paving slabs (1) enhance the Mediterranean feel with their texture and warm terracotta color. The one-turn flight of steps is faced with brick risers (2) and lit by a spotlight (3), placed low so as not to dazzle. The lower level is covered with gravel (4) and a circular pool, with a small fountain, is surrounded by bricks (5).

The old-world feel is continued in the stone sculpture (6) and in the classic design of the garden furniture (7). The aluminium table and chairs retain the elegant Victorian style and wrought-iron look.

The reconstituted stone urns (8, 9) are also in the classic style, one filled with begonias and geraniums, the other with daisylike marguerites. The maple tree (10), in its decorative wooden box, will turn crimson in the fall. Alpine strawberries (11) soften the line of the stone steps. A raised bed, of alpine plants and grasses, is retained by a dry-stone wall (12). Other plants include Livingstone daisies (13), water lilies and the flowering rush *Butomus umbellatus* (14) and, with conservation in mind, a tub of wild flowers (15), grown from seed.

that, when the flowering season is over, you still have something attractive to look at. Climbing evergreen clematis, upright dwarf conifers such as golden chamaecyparis, or prostrate creeping ceanothus or juniper – plants like these give interest throughout the year.

If your patio is situated directly off the living room, continue the design of that room outside by linking the color scheme, for example, of the furnishings with your potted plants or the architectural shape of your houseplants with those outdoors. Palms, ferns, monsteras, fatsias – all can do well in summer on a patio. Bamboo, pampas grass or the wild festuca grasses are wonderful for adding delicacy and sculptural form.

Strings of fairy lights or well-placed spotlights can turn this outdoor living room into a magical place on a mild summer evening. It is important to get an electrician to do this job professionally, since the electrical circuit must be isolated, fully insulated and sealed.

Another delight of a patio, especially if it is sunny and enclosed, is growing herbs and scented shrubs. Lavender, rosemary, mint and many others can be grown easily in tubs or raised beds, as can jasmine, honeysuckle, evening primrose, night-scented stock and Banksia roses, where hardy.

THE INFORMAL PATIO GARDEN

Altogether different from the old-world look of the terrace garden opposite is this modern functional deck. Once again, good design has made the most of the area, with a split-level plan and wide steps leading down to the lower area. Mixing wooden planks with concrete slabs gives texture relief.

Redwood and red cedar are the only timbers that do not need preserving treatment.

To stop the surface becoming slippery, decking should be scrubbed down in spring and fall with salt or a proprietary cleaner, roughed up with a wire brush and then hosed down.

Split-level decking (**1**) mixed with precast concrete slabs (**2**) form this patio floor. The colored slabs relieve the wood finish. Choose colors to blend in with your home, containers and plants.

A wooden pergola (**3**) fulfils several functions on a patio. It provides shelter and shade in the sitting area, here furnished with a pair of comfortable lawn chairs (**4**). Spotlights (**5**) hang from the beams. Climbers like grape vines or honeysuckle, their roots in deep soil, can be trained from a wall trellis (**6**) over a pergola. Wooden shelving (**7**) attached to the uprights will hold pots or seedlings.

Different shaped containers add interest. Bright, modular plastic units are planted with lettuce (**8**); a square box with sculptural dwarf conifers (**9**); a round pot of begonias (**10**); a large wooden tub of scented herbs, such as lavender and thyme (**11**); and pots of miniature roses (**12**). A reconstituted stone trough (**13**), filled with wet peat, provides the right conditions for marginal water plants such as marsh marigolds and beardless irises. Always keep their roots in 2–3 inches of water.

Backyard steps provide a good sunny spot for pots of chrysanthemum and geranium. Winter-flowering

Elegance and simplicity are apparent in this charming display outside a town house. The narrow paved area complements the brickwork of the walls. The white plastic containers were chosen for their geometric look, their straight sides reflecting the other angles of the setting. The flowers themselves tumble from the urns, in matching arrangements of red geraniums, white petunias and blue hanging lobelia. This is an unfussy display, well thought-out yet informal, the whole effect inviting you up the steps to the door.

Verbena overflows from a square wooden box container, set on the steps of a paved patio. Wooden containers (unless specially seasoned) can rot easily so they should be raised off the ground on blocks to let air circulate beneath them. Verbena is a versatile pot plant. Not only does it flower prolifically throughout the summer, but it also has a lovely fragrance.

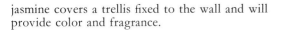

jasmine covers a trellis fixed to the wall and will provide color and fragrance.

A floral sculpture, this cascade of busy lizzies makes an impressive display and is surprisingly easy to create. A tall planter made from plastic or terracotta can be bought at the garden center. Fill it with moistened potting mix, then water thoroughly and compact the soil. Seedlings are planted through the holes; angle them slightly outward as if you were planting up the edge of a window box.

CONTAINER PLANTS: BASIC CARE

All container-grown plants, both indoors and out, are dependent on their owners. Try to establish a regular care routine and make your "maintenance plan" as easy as possible to carry out. In this way you are less likely to be tempted to "procrastinate" or take short cuts. The rewards of meticulous and routine care will be evident in your thriving plants.

Soil

The great advantage of container growing is that it is possible to provide individual plants with almost exactly the soil they require. Potting mixes come in a variety of strengths, graded to different stages of growth; choose one that is appropriate for the age and type of plant, bearing in mind that specially formulated mixes are available for lime and acid lovers. (The "ericaceous" mixes are best suited to heathers, rhododendrons and azaleas, the acid lovers.)

As well as containing the right acid or lime level for a particular plant, potting mixes must be crumbly in texture, able to retain moisture without becoming waterlogged, allow for easy drainage and free air circulation, and contain the correct balance of nutrients.

Ordinary garden soil, apart from carrying the danger of possible infestation with disease organisms or insect pests, is not always able to meet all these requirements.

Choose a reliable brand of standard potting mix, from a source which you know has a quick turnover, since mixes deteriorate with age. If you have to store unopened bags at home, make sure they are kept in a frost-free place and in very cold weather take them indoors for a couple of days to allow them to warm up before use.

Besides the standard loam-based mix ("loam," incidentally, simply means good quality soil), soilless mixes are also obtainable. These are generally peat-based, cheaper, lighter and cleaner than loam-based kinds. (Azaleas and other acid lovers do particularly well in the peat-based mixes.) However, plants do not establish so firm a root hold in soilless mixes and while lightness may be an advantage in hanging baskets or window boxes, it is a disadvantage in containers with large plants, where weight goes hand in hand with stability.

For most purposes, a half-and-half mix of loam- and peat-based kinds is likely to provide an acceptable solution.

Watering

Make watering less of a chore by using as capacious a watering can as you are able to carry easily (2 gallons is about right for most people), with a long spout and sprinkler rose head. If you have a large number of plants to attend to, it makes sense to invest in a hose, to eliminate endless trips to the faucet for refilling. Even balcony gardeners will find a hose useful. If you don't have one, an outdoor faucet will make the whole process much easier.

How much water you give and when will depend on the time of year and the general weather conditions. In high summer once, twice or even more daily watering may be necessary, particularly in the case of hanging baskets. Preferably water in the early morning or early evening. Misting foliage and moistening the soil before the sun comes up in hot weather is an effective way of preventing wilting later in the day. A mulch of bark chips, held down by heavier gravel pieces in areas exposed to the wind, will also help delay drying out.

It is essential to water thoroughly. Wait until water begins to emerge from the bottom of the container; and if this happens too quickly do not be content with one watering. Peat-based mixes in particular are prone to form a "crust" around the root ball, so water until you are sure this has been penetrated.

During brief holiday absences container plants can be provided for in much the same way as indoor plants. Capillary mats, drip-feed arrangements, plastic bag covers will all help retain moisture for a short period. If you can afford them, self-watering troughs or window boxes are another solution. For longer absences it will be necessary to engage a plant sitter or enlist help from a friendly neighbor.

Winter watering depends on situation and climate zone: in most temperate zones, two to three times a month should be adequate.

Feeding

Regular feeding is essential for container-grown plants as they will quickly use up the nutrients available to them in most standard potting mixes. In the case of soilless mixes it will be necessary to begin feeding after about six weeks; in the case of loam-based mixes nutrients will need supplementing after about two months.

Slow-release fertilizers that provide nourishment for about two or three months are available in stick or granule form and seem to be the perfect answer, particularly for the forgetful gardener. It must be noted, however, that some specialists advise against their use because they believe it may lead to a build-up of salts that could inhibit plant growth.

Quick-acting, water-soluble fertilizers should be applied during the plant's growing period. Always water the soil before feeding. Do not feed during the plant's dormant period.

Containers

Plants will grow in all kinds of containers providing you give them the correct mixture of water, soil and light. Sometimes it is fun to use unusual receptacles, such as kitchen colanders, gallon-size drums, old gardening gloves, rubber boots, hollowed-out tree trunks, auto tires . . . the list depends on your ingenuity. But often the simpler, more traditional containers look best and are easiest to handle.

Your choice of container will depend first on the type of plant you have. You cannot, for example, put a vigorous passion flower or honeysuckle, with an extensive root system, into a 6-inch pot since, given the right conditions, it will burst out within the season, A group of alpine flowers or small desert cacti will be lost in a large tub – alpines are shallow-rooters and cacti like to be potbound. So first, you need to know the habits and needs of your plants.

Next, the space available for the containers, their setting and the effect you wish to create will dictate whether you buy, for example, classic terracotta urns, plastic pots, modular fiberglass units, reconstituted stone troughs or rustic wooden tubs. Your collection might, in fact, contain all of these since the different shapes, sizes, colors and textures lend interest to container gardening and also give a wider scope for matching your plants with your containers.

Choosing containers
When choosing containers, consider their depth, width, drainage facilities and overall durability. Keep weight in mind also if you are placing them on a balcony or window ledge. Different shapes are useful, such as triangular boxes for corners or hexagonal units which can interlock in interesting designs. Color is another consideration; neutral colors are often best since it is usually the plants you want noticed, not the containers. Dark-colored pots absorb and retain heat and are good to give seedlings a fast start or for tomatoes or peppers which like warmth.

Drainage holes are provided in most manufactured containers. Before adding the potting mix, put a layer of clay shards over the holes, followed perhaps with a layer of leaf mold, to keep the soil well drained and fresh. If you have to drill holes, make them at least a half inch in diameter and 6 inches apart. On very level surfaces, such as paving slabs, it is wise to lift your containers off the ground on low blocks, so that air can circulate beneath and water can drain away easily.

Most containers need some kind of preparation. Wooden tubs, window boxes or old beer barrels, for example, should be treated inside with a safe

A simple basket, acting as an outer container, gives this arrangement of petunias, marigolds and lobelia a rustic look, complemented by the warm brickwork of the patio. The flowers are planted in a plastic pot, then placed in the basket. This has been lined with a layer of plastic so that excess water, dripping from the pots, will not come in contact with the wickerwork and cause it to rot.

timber preservative and coated on the outside with paint or varnish, so that they do not rot with time and exposure. Never use creosote since the fumes can be poisonous to plants. Metal window boxes will need treatment with an anti-rust paint. Plastic containers should be kept scrupulously clean since they do not "mellow" with age, but just look dirtier. Reconstituted stone containers, on the other hand, often become covered with a layer of moss or lichen and look better after a few years of weathering.

Terracotta pots come in all shapes and sizes, and are very handsome, if expensive. But they have the disadvantage of being porous and the soil, with its water and nutrients, can quickly dry out. Thus, unglazed clay pots need more attention than plastic ones. But you can have the advantages of both, by planting up in a plastic pot and slipping this into a slightly larger terracotta one for effect. Clay pots are also prone to damage by frost, but you can leave them out during the colder months if they are protected by a layer of insulating material. In extreme cold, plastic can become brittle and shatter.

An old porcelain or stone sink makes an ideal shallow container for rock plants. You can disguise it, or give it a "face lift," by painting on a bonding agent and, when this is dry, coating it with an artificial "antique stone" finish.

Since the great advantage of container gardening is movability, you can change your plants around to catch more light or shade, to adjust the levels of a group or to alter the color scheme.

There are various ways of moving heavy containers without straining your back. The first rule may be obvious – move the container *before* watering. An 18-inch wooden box with soil weighs 200 pounds and, with water, is considerably heavier. Besides mounting a heavy container on a dolly or a platform on casters, other methods include pulling it on a canvas bag or piece of carpet; sliding it along on a wide shovel; or rolling it over a series of poles, pipes or broom handles laid at regular intervals on the ground.

A sheltered area is ideal for plants that like plenty of light and warmth. But do remember to water, since the soil can dry out quickly in such conditions, especially through the porous walls of clay pots.

Geraniums are ideal flowers for a sunny terrace. They grow rapidly and by mid-summer, this decorative terracotta urn will be full of flowers.

TYPES OF CONTAINER

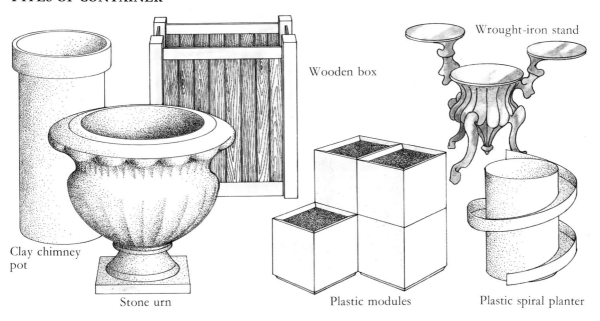

Clay chimney pot

Wooden box

Wrought-iron stand

Stone urn

Plastic modules

Plastic spiral planter

Houseplants outdoors

Many of the houseplants that are nurtured in the stable controlled conditions of our homes or garden rooms relish a spell outdoors in summer. Provided they are placed in a suitable situation, they will flourish on plenty of fresh air, natural light and rainwater, and return indoors the better for their "vacation."

Cacti and succulents, such as aloe, agave and crassula, should spend some time outdoors each year to be really healthy, top quality plants. Passion flowers, agapanthus and yuccas are among many others that thrive outside in summer and spider plants (*Chlorophytum comosum*), with their arching stems carrying tiny plantlets, are ideal for hanging baskets.

Move plants out to a balcony or patio once the weather has warmed up, perhaps to make attractive groupings with pots of summer annuals. Alternatively, plunge pots up to their rims in garden soil to keep them cool and moist. Do not assume that all tropical plants like basking in hot sun. Certain cacti, for example, grow on trees in their jungle home and must be placed in shade outdoors.

Take care when choosing which plants to move outside – some suggestions are included in the following pages. The tenderest species would not welcome the change in surroundings and conditions, and could be seriously damaged. Be sure, too, to move all indoor/outdoor plants back inside again well before there is any danger of frost. Check them over carefully before placing back into their permanent positions in case they have become infested with aphids or other pests. Keep such plants separate until the pests have been destroyed.

African blue lily

AGAPANTHUS AFRICANUS

A stately plant with strap-shaped leaves, the African blue lily bears delicate blue flowers on erect stems. When grown in pots and tubs it reaches a height of $1\frac{1}{2}$ to 2 feet and a spread of 2 to $2\frac{1}{2}$ feet. The plant is a member of the Liliaceae family.

Some varieties of agapanthus particularly worthy of note are *A. a. variegatus*, with white striped leaves, and *A. a. albidus*, which bears beautiful white flowers.

GREEN THUMB GUIDE

Watering
Water regularly, particularly in hot weather, but do not allow the soil to become waterlogged. After flowering, reduce the amount of water given and let the plant remain almost dry during its rest period. Increase watering again when growth resumes in spring.

Feeding
Feed every two weeks in the growing season with water-soluble fertilizer.

General care
Remove faded flowers and, once flowering has finished completely, remove stems as close to the base of the plant as possible.

CONTAINER CULTIVATION

Agapanthus is an ideal tall subject for a large container, with dimensions of at least 12 inches deep and 12–18 inches wide. In frost-free zones 9 and 10, it is hardy all year round. Elsewhere, it thrives on a summer outdoors in a bright sunny spot out of the wind. It must be taken indoors for the winter. It does not like its fleshy roots disturbed unduly, so do not repot until absolutely necessary. In fact, agapanthus flowers best when somewhat potbound.

Agave
AGAVE AMERICANA

A succulent from Mexico, agave is grown for its sword-shaped leaves which add a touch of drama to a collection of terrace plants. Container-grown agaves rarely bloom, but flowers are greenish-yellow and give out a delicate fragrance at night. In zones 7, 8, 9 and 10 (see p. 4) the agave can remain outdoors year round, but elsewhere it is best grown as a houseplant and moved outside for the summer months only. It belongs to the Agavaceae family.

Pot-grown agaves reach a height of 3 feet or more, the fleshy, spiny-edged leaves forming a rosette shape. A mature plant forms offsets at the base of the rosette and these can be used to raise new plants. Remove the offsets carefully, dry them out for a few days and plant in a standard potting mix. Agave can also be grown from seeds planted in spring at a temperature of about 70°F.

Given suitable conditions and treatment, agave is not a difficult plant to grow but may become infested by mealybugs. Watch out for the telltale patches of white waxy wool that cover a colony of these pests and spray thoroughly with a suitable insecticide.

Distinctive yellow stripes border the leaves of *A. a. marginata*, one of the most popular varieties of agave.

GREEN THUMB GUIDE

Containers
Tubs and large pots, at least 12 inches deep and 12 to 24 inches across, are best for the agave. Plant one agave to a container.

Position
Agave thrives in full sun while outdoors. In winter, keep at a minimum temperature of 41°F.

Soil
Use a standard houseplant potting mix.

Watering
Water freely during the summer but allow to dry out between waterings in winter.

Feeding
Feed every two weeks in the growing season with water-soluble fertilizer.

General care
Repot the agave every three or four years in spring, removing any offshoots to make new plants.

Love-lies-bleeding

AMARANTHUS CAUDATUS

Plumelike spikes of tiny red flowers bloom throughout the summer and make love-lies-bleeding a rewarding terrace plant.

Tassels of brilliant red flowers distinguish this native of tropical Asia which will thrive on a sunny terrace for the summer months. In other than frost-free zones it must be taken back into a cool room or greenhouse in fall since it is extremely sensitive to frost. It can also be grown as an annual. Commonly known as love-lies-bleeding or the tassel flower, *Amaranthus caudatus* is a member of the Amaranthaceae family.

When container-grown, the plant reaches a height of 2 to 3 feet and a spread of 8 to 16 inches. Its erect habit makes it suitable both as the central feature of a group of lower-growing annuals and for growing alone. Its tiny red flowers are tightly packed on plumelike spikes up to 18 inches long and they continue to bloom throughout the summer. Leaves are oval and light- to mid-green.

Sow seeds directly into the container indoors. Once they are large enough to handle, thin to about 12 to 18 inches apart. Alternatively, sow seeds in a cold frame and plant out seedlings in late spring or early summer. Give plants some support since the flower heads become heavy as they develop.

GREEN THUMB GUIDE

Containers
Deep pots or tubs, at least 10 inches across, are best for this sizeable plant; shallow containers such as window boxes are not suitable. Plant one specimen per pot or group several, 10 inches apart, in larger containers.

Position
Place in a sheltered sunny spot, preferably with some shade for part of the day.

Soil
Use a light soil that is rich in humus and contains some lime.

Watering
In summer water as necessary – every day in hot weather. As the weather cools give the plant less water.

Feeding
Give water-soluble fertilizer every 10 days once the flower spikes appear.

Bellflower

CAMPANULA POSCHARSKYANA

A rampant, fast-growing campanula with a mass of purple-blue flowers, this species can be grown indoors or out in summer. Trailing in habit, it looks extremely attractive as an edging plant in a tub or box, or tumbling from a hanging basket. In winter, in other than frost-free zones, take the plant into a cool and bright position. Like all campanulas, the bellflower belongs to the Campanulaceae family.

The stems of this campanula may be as much as 2 feet long but, because they trail, the plant is actually only a few inches high. It spreads fast, however, to as much as 2 to 3 feet, so take care that it does not swamp other species planted nearby. Its pretty star-shaped flowers are $\frac{1}{2}$ to 1 inch across and bloom in profusion throughout the summer and well into fall in the south. The mid-green leaves, $1\frac{1}{2}$ inches long, are rounded in shape with toothed edges. Other rewarding plants are varieties of *C. carpatica*, with blue, purple or white flowers in late summer.

To raise your own plants, sow seeds in spring indoors. Once the seedlings are large enough to handle, transfer them to 3-inch pots until ready for planting out. The bellflower can also be propagated by division in spring. Although easy plants to grow, campanulas can be seriously damaged by slugs and snails which eat leaves and new shoots.

Tumbling cascades of lavender-blue, star-shaped flowers make the bellflower, *Campanula poscharskyana*, a rewarding plant to grow indoors or out.

GREEN THUMB GUIDE

Containers
Suitable for tubs, pots, window boxes and hanging baskets, this campanula needs a container at least 6 inches deep and 6 to 8 inches across. Group several plants together for a striking mass of flowers.
Use a standard potting mix.

Position
Campanula does best in light shade but will tolerate full sun. It is important to keep it sheltered from rain when outdoors – drops of water can mark its petals. Move indoors in winter.

Watering
Water generously in summer, taking care not to splash the flowers, but allow the soil to dry out slightly between waterings. The plant will tolerate periods of drought. In winter water sparingly, increasing the amount given when growth resumes in spring.

Feeding
Feed every 2 weeks in the growing season with water-soluble fertilizer. Do not feed in winter.

General care
Deadhead flowers to encourage new blooms.

Lantana

LANTANA CAMARA

A small upright shrub from the West Indies, lantana is hardy in zones 8, 9 and 10 (see p. 4) but is also popular farther north as a greenhouse or indoor plant that can be moved outdoors in summer. It is a member of the Verbanaceae family.

White, yellow or pink tubular flowers bloom in summer and darken to deep-orange or red as they age. Flowers of more than one shade may thus appear on a plant at one time. The mid- to dark-green leaves are 2 to 6 inches long and elliptic in shape. A mature plant may reach a height of 1½ to 4 feet with a spread of 1 to 3 feet. Some particularly attractive varieties of lantana are 'Cloth of Gold', which bears yellow flowers, 'Snow Queen', with cool white flowers, and 'Rose Queen', with deep pink blooms.

Grow lantana from seed or propagate from cuttings. Take 3-inch cuttings in August and root them in a mix of equal parts of peat and sand at a temperature of about 60°F. Overwinter in 3-inch pots, containing standard potting mix, and move to the final containers in spring.

Mealybugs and greenhouse orthezias (small sucking insects like mealybugs) may infest lantanas. Spray with suitable insecticide at the first sign of problems.

Butterflies are attracted to the pretty flowers of the lantana which subtly change in shade as they age. Grow lantana singly or group several to brighten your terrace or home.

GREEN THUMB GUIDE

Containers
Lantanas are shrublike in form and need large pots or tubs. Mature specimens are effective planted alone while younger plants can be grouped two or three together in a large container.

Position
In areas other than zones 8, 9 and 10 keep lantana indoors and move outside in June to a sunny or semishaded position. In fall, take the plant inside again before there is any risk of frost and keep at a minimum temperature of 45°F, increasing to 55°F in spring.

Soil
A standard houseplant potting mix is suitable for lantana.

Watering
In summer water generously, but allow the soil to dry out between waterings. Keep the plant barely moist in winter, only increasing the watering when growth starts in spring.

Feeding
Apply water-soluble fertilizer every two weeks in the growing season. Do not feed during the winter rest period.

General care
Repot lantana every two years or so. For mature plants, prune main shoots back in February. Large plants will need staking to support their growth.

Flowering annuals

Easy to grow and prolific with their blooms, annual plants can turn any balcony or patio into a riot of color for the summer months. Most, other than the tallest species, can be successfully grown in containers such as troughs, tubs, pots and window boxes. The root systems of annuals are shallow so the restrictions of a container present no space problem, and their speed of growth provides rapid and varied displays.

An annual is a plant that goes through its entire life cycle in one year; it is sown, blooms abundantly and dies within this period. In nature the plants seed themselves as the flowers die and fall and they reemerge year after year.

For the gardener, seeds of most annuals are readily obtainable and simple to raise. Most are best started indoors or, ideally, in a greenhouse. Sow in early spring (late February or early March in temperate zones) to produce plants that are large and sturdy enough for planting out in early summer.

Seedlings grown indoors cannot be suddenly plunged outdoors, however; the shock of the change would be too great. Most will need two or three weeks of conditioning or hardening off first. The best way of doing this is to place plants in a cold frame for a week or two. Alternatively, simply take plants outside for a short period in the day and bring them in at night, gradually increasing the length of time they spend outside until they are thoroughly acclimatized to the new conditions.

In southern zones some plants grown as annuals elsewhere can be treated as perennials. Annuals may also be planted out earlier in such areas and have a longer flowering season.

Once annuals have been planted in their container homes they need little maintenance other than regular watering and feeding. Most will benefit from being deadheaded (the removal of faded blooms) which encourages new flowers.

Pots of annuals can be grown almost anywhere to enliven a garden of foliage plants, to bring a touch of country freshness to a city window sill or balcony, or to furnish an elegant patio. Climbing annuals, such as morning glory, can be planted in a tub to make a rapid, yet luxuriant screen. Most annuals like a sunny position but some, such as lobelias, thrive in semi-shade. Geraniums, marigolds, verbenas and zinnias stand up well to heat and are good choices for south-facing window boxes. Annuals can also be used in hanging baskets. Ageratum, alyssum, lobelia, Livingstone daisy, geraniums, petunias and nasturtiums are all particularly suitable.

Using fragrant flowering plants can make containers even more delightful. Plant a window box of scented sweet alyssum, stocks and nicotiana.

Be imaginative when planting your container. Geraniums and petunias are justifiably popular, but they are not the only suitable annuals. Try salvia, black-eyed Susan, dahlias and others suggested in the following pages. Try combining several plants in a pot or box – having first checked that they will thrive under similar conditions.

Above: The familiar, fast-growing, vining-type nasturtium (*Tropaeolum majus*) can be planted to trail from a pot or hanging basket or to clamber up a support. It bears bright orange, yellow or red blooms throughout summer.

Left: Annual chrysanthemums, such as *Chrysanthemum × spectabile*, produce abundant flowers and are suitable for large pots and tubs.

Below: The fluffy clusters of flowers of *Ageratum houstonianum* are usually blue, but there are also pink and white varieties. Ageratum combines well with taller plants such as geraniums and snapdragons.

Below left: The Livingstone daisy (*Dorotheanthus bellidiformis*) forms dense mats of tiny colorful flowers, ideal for edging boxes or tubs.

Snapdragon
ANTIRRHINUM MAJUS

Glossy-green leaves and colorful spikes of long-lasting flowers make the snapdragon or antirrhinum an excellent choice for containers and window boxes. The blooms, with their characteristic rounded upper and lower lips, may be white, pink, red, yellow or orange and open in sequence from bottom to top of the spike. Snapdragons belong to the Scrophulariaceae family.

Bushy dwarf varieties of snapdragon, which are only 4 to 6 inches high and spread 6 to 12 inches, are ideal for pots and boxes. Standard plants up to 2 feet tall can also be used for larger containers. Use snapdragons alone or combine them with other plants such as petunias, ageratum and campanula.

Sow snapdragon seeds indoors in early spring in a standard, peat-based mix. The seeds need light if they are to germinate, and must be kept moist but not wet. Move the seedlings to 3-inch pots when they are large enough to handle, and harden off outside for two weeks or so before planting in containers. Pinch out the tops of seedlings to keep the plants bushy; this is particularly important for the taller varieties.

Snapdragons are prone to rust. Grow the new rust-resistant strains, or spray the plants with fungicide. Aphids sometimes infest snapdragons, and tarnished plant bugs sting the buds and may destroy flowers. Treat the affected plants with an appropriate insecticide.

GREEN THUMB GUIDE

Containers
Pots, tubs and window boxes at least 12 inches wide and 6 inches deep are suitable for growing snapdragons. Dwarf varieties are best for window boxes and all but the largest pots.

Position
Snapdragons thrive in a warm sunny place but prefer to be shaded from the hottest midday sun. They tolerate deeper shade but will produce fewer flowers.

Soil
Use a standard potting mix or a mixture containing sand and rich compost.

Watering
Water daily in hot weather, less often at other times. Snapdragons will tolerate short periods of drought.

Feeding
Apply water-soluble fertilizer every two weeks once the flower spikes appear.

China aster
CALLISTEPHUS CHINENSIS

Beautiful, daisylike flowers in glowing shades of pink, red and purple make the China aster one of the most popular annuals. Many varieties are now available with single and double flowers ranging in size from $1\frac{1}{2}$ to 5 inches across. Leaves are about 3 inches long and widely toothed. Standard China asters are up to 2 feet high but dwarf varieties of 10 to 12 inches tall, with a spread to 8 to 10 inches, are best for containers.

China asters are probably best planted on their own, partly because their colors are so vibrant but also because they are prone to several diseases such as wilt, mildew and yellows. New varieties are now available that are resistant to wilt, and mildew can be controlled with fungicide.

Yellows can be more serious. It is a viral disease spread by the six-spotted leaf hopper and causes yellowed foliage and stunted growth. Badly affected plants should be destroyed to avoid spread of the disease. Pests such as blister beetles and aphids can also be a hazard. Despite these problems, China asters grow well with good care.

Sow seeds indoors in spring. When the seedlings are large enough to handle, transplant them into small pots. Use sterilized soil to reduce likelihood of spreading wilt. Harden off outside for a week or two before transferring to final position. After risk of frost has passed, plant seeds outside for late summer and fall blooms.

GREEN THUMB GUIDE

Position
China asters do well in full sun, even in hot weather, but do like some shelter from wind. They tolerate light shade.

Soil
Use a standard potting mix or a sandy soil with added organic material. Be sure to use fresh soil every year since wilt can live in the mix. Sow seeds in sterilized soil.

Watering
Water freely, particularly in hot weather. Do not allow the soil to remain excessively wet for long periods, since this may encourage wilt.

Feeding
Apply water-soluble fertilizer every 10 days once the flower buds show.

General care
Remove faded flowers to encourage new blooms. Allow plants plenty of air space – cramped conditions may encourage disease.

Cathedral bell
COBAEA SCANDENS

Also known as the cup-and-saucer vine, the cathedral bell is a vigorous climbing plant which clings to a support with strong, pealike tendrils. Bell-shaped, purple flowers hang gracefully from foot-long stems amid a mass of twining foliage. The plant is a member of the Polemoniaceae family.

A native of Mexico, the cathedral bell can be grown as a perennial in zones 9 and 10 (see p. 4) but elsewhere is treated as an annual. Even in a container this incredibly fast-growing plant can reach a height of 10 feet or more and makes a perfect choice when a rapid screen is needed to disguise an ugly fence or wall. Because of its vigor, it is best grown alone and not combined with other plants.

Cobaea does not flower until it has grown 5 feet or more so must be started early. To grow it as an annual, sow seeds indoors in February or March. Sow one to a pot, cover with glass or plastic, and keep at a temperature of about 64°F. Pot on as necessary, using twigs to support growth, and harden off for two weeks before planting out.

GREEN THUMB GUIDE

Containers
This vigorous plant needs a large pot or tub at least 12 inches deep and 18 to 24 inches across.

Position
A sunny, sheltered location against a south- or west-facing wall is ideal. Cobaea does tolerate shade but flowers less profusely.

Soil
Use a light sandy soil. If the soil is too rich the plant produces too much foliage at the expense of flowers.

Watering
Water generously, especially in hot weather. Periods of drought will slow down the plant's growth.

Feeding
Apply water-soluble fertilizer every two weeks during the growth period.

TRELLIS SUPPORT
Cobaea is such a vigorous climber that it can quickly get untidy and out of hand, even when its roots are restricted within a container. Keep this vine tidy by encouraging it to grow up a trellis. Since it will cling tenaciously to the support by means of its tendrils there is rarely any need to tie the stems to the trelliswork. A trellis-trained vine such as this looks well against the wall of any house or garage.

A fast-growing climbing plant, *Cobaea scandens* rapidly
creates a decorative screen of luxuriant foliage and
delicate flowers that are greenish-yellow on opening,
turning to purple. Each bloom has petals arranged in
a bell-shape, surrounded by saucer-like sepals.

Dahlia

DAHLIA × CULTORUM

Like their taller relatives, dwarf bedding dahlias bear showy, brilliantly colored flowers but their smaller size makes them ideally suited to pots and boxes. Most dwarf varieties are 12 to 20 inches tall with a spread of about 12 inches. Flowers are 1 to 4 inches across in many shades of pink, red, lilac, yellow and orange, and are single, double or semidouble depending on variety. In most zones they will bloom from midsummer to fall.

Sow seeds indoors in early spring. Dahlias are very susceptible to frost damage so transplant the strongest seedlings to their outdoor homes only when all danger of frost is past.

Dahlias are prone to attack by aphids at all stages of growth, so spray with pesticide to keep the problem under control. Caterpillars may also attack plants, eating leaves and tunneling into the stems.

Viruses, gray mold and petal blight often affect dahlias, dwarfing and distorting their growth. Treat with the appropriate fungicide or destroy badly affected plants to avoid spread of the disease.

Despite all these problems dahlias are still wonderful plants to grow and with good care survive the summer well.

Dwarf dahlias, available in a wonderful array of flower types and colors, enhance any container and bloom throughout the summer.

GREEN THUMB GUIDE

Containers
These small dahlias look splendid in all sorts of tubs, pots and troughs and in window boxes. Containers should be at least 6 to 8 inches deep. Plant dahlias in groups of three to five, or combine them with other plants such as nemesias.

Position
A sunny location suits dahlias best, but they will grow reasonably well in shade.

Soil
Use a standard potting mix. Use fresh soil each year to be sure that it is free from disease.

Watering
Water plants thoroughly every day in hot weather. At other times allow the soil to dry out slightly between waterings. Plants in shady places need less water than those situated in full sun.

Feeding
Apply water-soluble fertilizer once or twice only during the growing season. Too much encourages leaf growth at the expense of flowers.

General care
Deadhead the plants regularly to encourage new flowers.

Cape marigold

DIMORPHOTHECA SINUATA

A South African plant with daisylike flowers, the Cape marigold thrives in hot dry situations, so is a particularly useful plant for warmer zones. It can be grown as a perennial in the south but should be treated as an annual in the north.

The Cape marigold's narrow leaves are about 3 inches long with toothed edges, and its flowers are orange, yellow or white depending on variety. The plant reaches a height of about 12 inches.

For annual plants, sow seeds indoors in early spring and transfer young plants outside once there is no danger of frost.

GREEN THUMB GUIDE

Containers
Plant in tubs, pots, troughs or window boxes. The white variety makes an attractive companion to brighter flowers such as petunias or geraniums.

Position
The flowers of the Cape marigold open only in sun so, to look its best, the plant must be in a sunny location.

Soil
Use standard potting mix.

Watering
Water regularly, but allow the soil to dry out slightly between waterings.

Feeding
Apply water-soluble fertilizer every two weeks once the flower buds have formed.

General care
Remove faded blooms promptly.

California poppy
ESCHSCHOLZIA CALIFORNICA

The California poppy opens its glowing yellow flowers, flushed with orange, only in sunny weather and from mid-morning to late afternoon. The saucer-shaped blooms, 2 to 3 inches across, fade rapidly but new ones quickly take their place, keeping the plant in flower until fall. About 12 to 16 inches in height, with a spread of 6 inches, the plant has finely-cut, blue-green leaves.

Varieties of the California poppy are available with single or double flowers in yellow, orange and red and there are compact forms such as 'Mission Bells' which are only 9 inches high. These low-growing plants are particularly suitable for window boxes and smaller containers.

Because the California poppy has a tap root (like that of a carrot) it does not react well to disturbance and transplanting. Sow seeds directly into containers where they are to grow and thin out once established. Seeds take only about 14 days to germinate, and the plant is generally free of pests and diseases.

A fast-growing member of the poppy family Papaveraceae, the California poppy is ideal for filling a gap in a container of slower-growing, later-blooming plants. It stands up well to intense heat and will even tolerate periods of drought.

GREEN THUMB GUIDE

Containers
California poppies can be planted in any sort of tub, trough or pot, alone or combined with other annuals. Use dwarf varieties in window boxes.

Position
The flowers do not open in shade, so place the plant in full sun.

Soil
Light sandy soil will produce the best flowers. Too rich a soil encourages foliage at the expense of flowers.

Watering
Water generously but allow the soil to dry out between waterings. The plant will tolerate periods of drought.

Feeding
Feed once or twice only during the growing season with water-soluble fertilizer.

Candytuft
IBERIS UMBELLATA

Clusters of tiny flowers adorn the pretty candytuft which blooms through summer into fall. An erect branching plant, it grows to about 6 to 12 inches tall with a spread of 6 to 8 inches. Its pointed narrow leaves are 2 to 3 inches long. Two attractive varieties are 'Dwarf Fairy', which has white, lilac or pink blooms, and 'Rose Cardinal', with rose-red flowers. Try using candytuft to provide interest at the base of climbing plants such as morning glory or black-eyed Susan.

Sow candytuft seeds indoors in early spring. Keep seedlings at 40°F to 50°F and harden off for a week or two outdoors before planting out into containers. Make several successive sowings and have new plants available when the first batch cease to bloom.

Seeds can be sown directly into containers and thinned to a distance of about 8 inches apart. Whatever method is used, do not place plants outside until all danger of frost is past.

A member of the mustard family Cruciferae, candytuft is easy to grow and needs little attention other than regular deadheading to prolong the flowering period. It is a good choice for a city balcony since it tolerates urban dirt and fumes well.

GREEN THUMB GUIDE

Containers
Plant candytuft in pots, low tubs and window boxes which are at least 10 inches across and 6 inches deep. Mix them with other plants or plant in groups about 8 inches apart.

Position
A sunny location is best. Candytuft does tolerate shade but flowers less profusely out of the sun.

Soil
Candytuft grows well even on poor soil but a sandy mix suits it best.

Watering
Water regularly during the growing period but do not allow the soil to become waterlogged. Mature plants will tolerate dry periods.

Feeding
Apply water-soluble fertilizer every two weeks once the flower buds show some color.

Morning glory

IPOMOEA TRICOLOR

An attractive climber, morning glory bears pink, mauve or blue trumpet-shaped flowers which bloom in the morning and fade by afternoon. Fortunately, the flowers are as prolific as they are short-lived. The twining stems with their pretty, heart-shaped leaves reach 7 to 10 feet, with a spread of 2 to 4 feet. Given some support such as wire or trellis they rapidly create an effective screen. Use several plants together for the best display since they are fairly slender in habit. A sunny sheltered position is best, against a south-facing wall. These plants are members of the Convolvulaceae family, which includes the ubiquitous bindweed.

Sow seeds indoors in early spring, having first soaked them overnight or chipped the outer covering to aid germination. Place 2 or 3 seeds to a pot, and when the seedlings are about 2 inches tall, remove all but the strongest plants. Even at this stage seedlings need some form of support such as twigs or small stakes. Wait until the weather has definitely warmed up before planting outside, having allowed for 2 weeks of hardening-off first.

GREEN THUMB GUIDE

Containers
Use tubs or pots at least 12 inches deep and 10 to 16 inches across, and provide adequate support for this vigorous climber.

Soil
Use a light lime-free soil. Too rich a soil encourages leaves not flowers.

Watering
Water generously in hot weather, less at other times. Do not allow the soil to remain waterlogged since this can cause root rot.

Feeding
Apply water-soluble fertilizer every two weeks once flower buds show.

Herb tree-mallow
LAVATERA TRIMESTRIS

An erect bushy plant, the herb tree-mallow bears pink, funnel-shaped flowers from mid- to late summer. The blooms have an attractive satiny texture and are reminiscent of hollyhock flowers. Like the hollyhock, the herb tree-mallow belongs to the Malvaceae family.

The plant reaches a height of 2 to 3 feet and a spread of up to 16 inches. Leaves are rounded and slightly lobed. Some particularly attractive varieties of lavatera are 'Mont Blanc' with white flowers; 'Loveliness' with deep rose-pink; and 'Silver cup' with pink flowers marked with delicate silver lines.

Sow seeds of this hardy annual in late spring and thin out after four weeks. Do not keep the seedlings indoors since too much warmth causes the plants to become thin and leggy.

Although an easy plant to grow, mallow can be badly affected by rust, which causes raised orange patches on stems and leaves, and by leaf spot, which shows as yellow-brown spots on leaves and stems. Treat promptly with the appropriate fungicide before too much of the plant is damaged.

GREEN THUMB GUIDE

Containers
Pots and tubs at least 12 inches wide and 8 inches deep are best for this sizeable plant. Group 3 or more specimens together, placing them 6 to 8 inches apart.

Position
Place in a sunny but sheltered site or in light shade with sun for half of the day.

Soil
A light standard mix is best for the herb tree-mallow; too rich a soil encourages excessive leaf growth.

Watering
Water generously in hot weather, less at other times. Do not allow the soil to remain waterlogged.

Feeding
Apply water-soluble fertilizer every two weeks once the flower buds show color.

Monkey flower

MIMULUS LUTEUS

Yellow tubular flowers spotted with red or purple markings adorn the monkey flower, which is a native of Chile. It resembles the snapdragon and is a member of the same family, Scrophulariaceae. Some forms of this plant are only 6 inches tall, others as much as 2 feet, so it is important to check on the height of your particular variety before selecting a container.

Sow seeds indoors in early spring and keep at 55°F to 60°F. When seedlings are large enough to handle, transplant the strongest to 3-inch pots and harden them off for a few weeks before transferring to containers in early summer.

POOLSIDE PLANTING

GREEN THUMB GUIDE

Position
A sunny location with some shelter from the wind is best, but the monkey flower will also grow well in shade.

Soil
Use a standard potting mix.

Watering
Water young seedlings sparingly; too much water may damage them. Once in containers, plants should be watered generously, but allow the soil to dry out slightly between waterings. Some species can actually live in water.

Feeding
Apply water-soluble fertilizer every two weeks once flower buds show.

Left: *Mimulus luteus* can grow as a marginal plant on a shallow shelf at the edge of a pool. It will tolerate about 3 inches of water covering its roots. *M. ringens*, with lavender-blue flowers, is a truly aquatic species, growing in up to 6 inches of water.
Below: Similar to *M. luteus*, *M. variegatus* has larger flowers; 'Queen's Prize' is a dwarf variety which blooms profusely during the summer months.

Nemesia
NEMESIA STRUMOSA

Profuse colorful flowers, often with contrasting or spotted throats, make nemesia a much-loved annual. Blooms may be up to one inch across and are tubular in shape with pouched bases; they grow in clusters and, depending on the variety, are white, lavender, pink, scarlet or yellow. The light-green leaves are lance-shaped with toothed edges. Some attractive varieties of nemesia are 'Blue Gem' with lavender-blue flowers, 'Fire King' with bright red blooms, and 'Suttonii', an improved variety with large flowers in a wide range of colors.

An erect, slightly bushy plant, nemesia grows to a height of 8 to 12 inches, with a spread of 6 inches or so. Dwarf varieties such as 'Nana Compacta' are perfect for window boxes where they combine well with nasturtiums, lobelias and dwarf dahlias.

Sow the seeds indoors in early spring and keep at about 60°F. Transfer the strongest seedlings to pots and harden them off outside for a week or two before setting in final containers after all danger of frost is past.

Not generally susceptible to many pests, nemesia may be prone to fungal root rot, which eventually causes the plants to collapse. Protection is easier than cure for this disease, which rarely occurs in well-tended plants. Nemesia belongs to the Scrophulariaceae family, like the snapdragon.

GREEN THUMB GUIDE

Containers
Use nemesia in tubs, pots and window boxes with a minimum depth of 6 to 8 inches. Plant in groups of 5 or more.

Position
Nemesia grows well in sun or light shade but cannot stand extreme heat. In the south it is probably best in semishade.

Soil
Use light to medium, slightly acid soil, containing plenty of organic matter.

Watering
Water generously particularly in hot dry spells. While lack of water produces weak spindly plants, over-wet soil can lead to fungal rot.

Feeding
Apply water-soluble fertilizer every two weeks once flower buds show.

Flowering tobacco
NICOTIANA ALATA

Grow flowering tobacco in window boxes or containers near the house so its sweet fragrance can be easily appreciated. An erect plant, it combines well with lower-growing annuals such as petunias. Try planting a terracotta pot with an all-white selection of nicotiana, petunias and campanulas for a cool, stylish effect.

A graceful plant which gives off a delightful fragrance at dusk, flowering tobacco looks well in a container with lower-growing plants.

Nicotiana normally grows to a height of about 2 feet with a spread of 12 to 18 inches. Its arching stems bear flaring, tubular flowers in white, pale green, red or pink, and large, slightly sticky leaves. Normally the flowers open only in the evening, not in sunshine, but new varieties have been developed that open day and night.

Sow seeds indoors in early spring. Do not cover since the seeds need light in order to germinate. Harden off outside for a week or two before planting out after frost. In the south this annual may succeed as a perennial.

GREEN THUMB GUIDE

Containers
Use tubs, troughs, pots or window boxes which are at least 8 inches deep and a foot across. Plant nicotiana in combination with other plants or in groups of three, spaced 12 inches apart. Dwarf varieties are best for window boxes and these all have daytime-opening flowers.

Position
Flowering tobacco plants grow well in sun or shade. In shady locations the flowers will open earlier in the day, not just in the evening.

Soil
Use a standard potting mix.
Too-rich soil is inclined to make them leafy

Watering
Water the plants generously in hot weather, but give less water at other times. Allow the soil to dry out slightly between waterings.

Feeding
Apply water-soluble fertilizer every two weeks once the flower buds have appeared.

General care
Remove faded flowers promptly to stimulate the formation of new flower buds.

Geranium

PELARGONIUM × HORTORUM

Perhaps the most popular of all container plants, geraniums flower for months in all sorts of pots, boxes and baskets. They are easy to care for and mix well with other plants such as dusty miller, lobelia, alyssum and lavender.

Zonal pelargoniums are the most familiar of these plants popularly, but incorrectly, known as geraniums. There are many varieties all with clusters of small flowers in white and shades of red and pink. The light- to mid-green leaves are rounded and usually bear characteristic bronze or maroon markings.

Although actually perennials, zonal pelargoniums can be grown as annuals from seed. Sow indoors or best of all, in a greenhouse, in early spring and keep at a temperature of 60°F to 64°F. When the seedlings are large enough to handle, transfer them to small pots to grow on. Plant out once all danger of frost is past. Alternatively, grow new plants from 4-inch stem cuttings taken in summer from the previous year's plants.

Geraniums are susceptible to conditions such as gray mold, rust and virus diseases. Treat accordingly, but destroy badly affected plants to prevent spread of the disease.

GREEN THUMB GUIDE

Position
A sunny location is best, in fact the more light, the better the flowers and the longer their season. Direct sunlight is essential.

Soil
Use standard potting mix.

Watering
Water regularly, but avoid overwatering which can damage the plants. Let the soil dry out between waterings. Reduce frequency in winter.

Feeding
Apply water-soluble fertilizer several times during the growth period.

General care
Deadhead regularly and pinch out tips to keep plants bushy. Prune in early spring.

Penstemon

PENSTEMON × GLOXINIOIDES

A hybrid of a Mexican species *P. hartwegii*, this tender penstemon is best grown as an annual in all but southern regions. The plant grows to a height of 9 to 18 inches and spread of up to a foot and bears two-lipped, trumpet-shaped flowers in shades of red, deep pink and purple. Like the snapdragon, penstemon is a member of the Scrophulariaceae family.

Grow penstemon from seed or from cuttings taken from mature plants. In frost-free zones, where penstemon can be grown as a perennial, divide clumps in spring to make new plants.

Spikes of scarlet flowers adorn this penstemon, a tender plant that grows well in containers. There are several recommended varieties, all with 1½ to 2-inch flowers, including 'Ruby King', 'Firebird' and 'Garnet,' with deep-red to scarlet flowers; 'King George' and 'Pennington Gem' are both crimson varieties, with white in the throats of the flowers.

GREEN THUMB GUIDE

Containers
Plant penstemon in large pots or tubs together with other summer annuals.

Position
A sunny location is best for penstemon, although it will also grow in light shade. It does best in a slightly moist atmosphere and may wilt in excessively dry heat.

Soil
Use a standard potting mix. Ensure it is well drained since these plants dislike wet conditions.

Watering
Water penstemons generously, but allow the soil to dry out slightly between waterings.

Feeding
Apply water-soluble fertilizer every two weeks during the growing season.

General care
Pinch out growing tips to encourage bushy branching growth.

Petunia

PETUNIA × HYBRIDA

With their showy, brilliantly colored flowers, petunias are popular plants for all sorts of containers from tubs to hanging baskets. The flaring, trumpet-shaped blooms are pink, purple, magenta, red, yellow or white and there are even new varieties with striped flowers. The leaves are pale-green and have a slightly sticky surface.

Petunias grow 8 to 16 inches tall and, with their curving branching stems, may spread 12 inches or more. The many varieties are grouped according to flower size and type. 'Multiflora' petunias are bushy and bear 2 to 3-inch flowers. 'Grandiflora' bear fewer larger flowers, which are up to 5 inches across and often frilled. 'Multiflora doubles' have double flowers which are 2 to 3 inches across. There are also 'Pendula' or trailing varieties which look particularly decorative in window boxes or hanging baskets, and dwarf plants just 6 inches or so high.

Plants are easily available in garden stores or can be grown from seed. Sow seeds in early spring in fine soil. The seed is too tiny to cover but should be pressed down well and watered. Cover the pots or boxes with glass or plastic or keep in a mini-propagator to aid germination. Be sure to harden-off young plants outside for a few weeks before transferring to containers once there is no danger of frost. With care, petunias will bloom from early summer through first frosts. Keep a check for whiteflies which may infest the undersides of leaves. Use an appropriate pesticide to clear.

GREEN THUMB GUIDE

Position

Petunias thrive in full sun but will grow in partial shade. Too much shade, however, will produce leggy straggly plants. Make sure plants are sheltered from wind or rain which can damage the flowers.

Soil

Use standard potting mix lightened with sand for good drainage. Too rich a soil encourages leaves rather than flowers.

Watering

Water regularly but with care. Too much water can cause the leaves to yellow.

Feeding

Apply water-soluble fertilizer every two weeks during the growing period.

General care

Remove faded flower heads regularly to encourage new blooms. Cut back straggly older stems in late summer to rejuvenate plants and encourage a second flush of flowers.

Harebell phacelia

PHACELIA CAMPANULARIA

A hardy annual that originates from southern California, harebell phacelia bears clusters of bright-blue, bell-shaped flowers from early to late summer. The flowers are about 1 inch across and seem particularly attractive to bees.

Phacelia's softly branching stems bear broad, dark-green leaves with irregularly toothed edges. A small bushy plant, it grows to a height of 9 inches or so and spreads about 6 inches. Plant several specimens together to produce a mass of flowers and foliage.

Sow seeds of the harebell phacelia outdoors in mid-April. Ideally, sow the seeds where they are to grow, since the plant does not take well to transplanting. Thin seedlings to 6 to 9 inches apart. In southern zones, seeds can be planted out earlier.

The plants are generally easy to grow and free of disease, but seedlings may be eaten by slugs.

GREEN THUMB GUIDE

Containers
All sorts of tubs and pots are suitable and phacelia can also be grown in window boxes. Group several plants together for the best effect. Containers should have a minimum depth of 6 to 8 inches.

Position
Phacelia grows well in sun or shade.

Soil
Use a standard potting mix with added sand since good drainage is essential.

Watering
Water generously, particularly in hot weather, but allow the soil to dry out partially between waterings.

Feeding
Apply water-soluble fertilizer every two weeks.

General care
Deadhead regularly to encourage new blooms.

Honeybees are attracted to the pretty blue flowers of the harebell phacelia with their long conspicuous stamens, loaded with yellow pollen.

Sage
SALVIA

Several varieties of salvia or sage make excellent container plants. Fiery red, scarlet sage is probably best planted alone while the daintier blue forms such as *S. farinacea* and *S. patens* make attractive displays with dusty miller and geraniums. Salvia is a member of the mint family, Labiatae.

Salvia grows 12 to 24 inches high and spreads up to 12 inches or so. Dwarf forms are available which are particularly suitable for container growing. An erect branching plant, salvia bears spikes of hooded tubular flowers which last for many weeks.

Mealycup sage, *Salvia farinacea*, bears tall spikes of small, tubular, purple-blue flowers.

Grow salvias as annuals in the north, but in frost-free zones treat them as perennials. For annual plants, sow seeds indoors in spring and plant out into containers once there is no danger of frost. Allow plants to harden off for a week or two before planting out.

GREEN THUMB GUIDE

Containers
Plant salvia in pots, tubs or window boxes which are at least 8 inches deep and 12 inches across. Group several together, 8 inches apart.

Position
Salvia thrives in full sunshine but will grow in partial shade.

Watering
Water generously in hot weather, but give less at other times. Allow the soil to dry out between waterings – if it is constantly wet the plant may suffer root rot.

Feeding
Apply water-soluble fertilizer every two weeks once the flower spikes are well developed.

General care
Deadhead by removing the whole flower stalk once all its blooms have faded.

The fiery red flower spikes of the eye-catching scarlet sage, *Salvia splendens*, are long-lasting. This handsome plant blooms right through summer until fall.

Butterfly flower

SCHIZANTHUS × WISETONENSIS

Also known as poor man's orchid, the butterfly flower bears profuse, orchidlike flowers in white and shades of pink, red and purple, all with yellowish markings at the throat. The delicate form of the bloom is thought to resemble a butterfly – hence the name.

The leaves of the butterfly flower are pale-green and deeply cut, giving them an almost feathery appearance. They have a slightly sticky surface. A compact but bushy plant, schizanthus grows up to 8 to 12 inches, with a spread of about 8 inches. Dwarf varieties are available which look pretty in small containers.

Schizanthus plants belong to the Solonaceae family, and this particular species is a hybrid of the Chilean *S. pinnatus* and *S. grahamii*.

Sow seeds in early spring indoors or under glass. Transfer the strongest seedlings to pots or boxes and harden off outside for several weeks before finally planting out in late spring for late summer blooms. In southern zones sow seed in fall for blooms the following spring. For good bushy plants, pinch out the tips of growing shoots and sideshoots. Aphids may infest schizanthus and it is also prone to fungal diseases such as crown and root rot, particularly if overwatered.

GREEN THUMB GUIDE

Containers
Plant the butterfly flower in pots, tubs or window boxes which should be at least 6 to 8 inches deep.

Position
A sunny location is best, but the plant will also grow well in partial shade. Provide shelter from wind which can damage the delicate flowers.

Watering
Water regularly, allowing the soil to dry out slightly between waterings. Avoid overwatering.

Feeding
Apply water-soluble fertilizer every two weeks.

General care
Provide stakes or other form of support for fully grown plants.

Dusty miller
SENECIO CINERARIA

Silvery-leaved senecio, commonly known as dusty miller, makes an admirable foil for brightly colored annuals and creates additional interest in any mixed window box or tub. Its deeply lobed leaves are covered with white woolly hairs which give the foliage an attractive silvery appearance. Try combining the plant with fuchsias or pretty pink geraniums for a charming, long-lasting display.

An upright bushy plant, senecio reaches a height of 1 to 2 feet and a spread of up to a foot. It bears small yellow flowers, each about 1 inch across, but these are insignificant compared to its foliage. One particularly handsome variety of senecio is *S. c. aureomarginatus* which has leaves bordered with yellow or orange. Senecio is a member of the Compositae family and native to southern Europe.

Grow senecio as a perennial in zones 7, 8, 9 and 10 (see p. 4), but elsewhere treat it as a half-hardy annual. Sow seeds indoors in March and set young plants outside after risk of frosts has passed. Perennial plants can also be propagated from cuttings.

Aphids sometimes infest senecio plants, causing their leaves to become sticky and checking growth. Senecio is also prone to powdery mildew, a fungus which deposits a white coating on the leaves. Treat these problems with the appropriate pesticide or fungicide respectively.

GREEN THUMB GUIDE

Containers
Plant senecio in any kind of pot, tub, trough or window box. It is also suitable for hanging baskets.

Position
A versatile plant, senecio grows well in sun or shade.

Soil
Use a standard potting mix.

Watering
Water generously as required, but do not allow the soil to remain waterlogged.

Feeding
Apply water-soluble fertilizer every two weeks.

General care
Pinch back growth to encourage the plant to produce new branches and to maintain a good bushy shape.

Black-eyed Susan
THUNBERGIA ALATA

A luxuriant climbing plant, black-eyed Susan bears flaring, trumpet-shaped flowers all summer long. The glowing orange blooms are about $1\frac{1}{2}$ inches across and have blackish-brown "eyes," hence the plant's common name. There is also a white variety T. a.'Alba,' and a yellow, T. a. 'Lutea,' both with dark centers.

The twining stems of thunbergia reach up to 5 or even 10 feet in length and bear 3-inch long mid-green leaves. Grow the plant round a window or let is wind gracefully around the handle of a basket or other support. It grows fast and soon provides a decorative profusion of flowers and foliage to screen an awkward looking wall or fence or to soften a facade.

A member of the Acanthaceae family, *Thunbergia alata* comes from the tropics and is a tender, half-hardy annual that needs careful looking after. Sow seeds indoors in early spring and cover the box or pots with glass or plastic to aid germination. As soon as some growth appears, move the pots into the light. Once the seedlings are 2 to 3 inches high, remove the glass or plastic from the pots.

Plant young specimens out once there is no danger of damage by frost. Provide adequate support, such as trellis or wire, for the thunbergia to climb on – it does not need to be tied. The first flowers should appear only eight weeks after sowing. An easy plant to grow, thunbergia is not generally susceptible to any pests or diseases.

GREEN THUMB GUIDE

Containers
Plant thunbergia in large pots, tubs or troughs with a depth of at least 8 inches, and provide it with some means of support such as trellis, wire or twigs. It can also be planted in a hanging basket and allowed to trail downward, or placed in a decorative basket where its stems can twine around the handle.

Position
This plant does well in semishade or full sun – a place against a south-facing wall is ideal. In southern zones plants may need some shelter from the hottest sun.

Soil
Use a standard potting mix.

Watering
Water generously, every day in hot weather. The soil should be kept moist and never allowed to dry out.

Feeding
Apply water-soluble fertilizer every two weeks once the plant is in bloom.

General care
Keep removing dead blooms to encourage new flowers to form.

Zinnia

ZINNIA ELEGANS

Bright daisylike blooms in a rainbow of colors adorn zinnias from midsummer to fall. Varieties are available with single or double flowers, ranging from 1 to 6 inches across, in white and many shades of pink, orange, yellow, scarlet and purple.

Zinnias grow to a height of 2 to 3 feet with a spread of up to a foot. Dwarf varieties, such as 'Lilliput' and 'Tom Thumb', are only 6 to 10 inches high and perfect for planting in window boxes and smaller containers. Lower-growing varieties should also be used in exposed situations since the taller flower stalks are fragile and easily damaged by wind or heavy rain. Zinnias originate from Mexico and are members of the Compositae family.

Because they are so vibrant in color, zinnias are best planted alone or combined solely with foliage plants. A further reason for keeping zinnias apart from other plants is that they are prone to virus diseases such as cucumber mosaic virus and tomato spotted wilt virus. These diseases cause plants to produce fewer blooms and those may be distorted and unattractive. Treat zinnias at the first sign of disease and destroy badly affected specimens. Mildew, too, can affect zinnias leaving white patches on foliage. Spray plants regularly with the appropriate fungicide to control this condition.

Sow seeds indoors or under glass. They germinate in only four or five days and grow fast but should not be transferred outside until all danger of frost is past. Alternatively, sow direct into outdoor containers after frost, then thin out and transplant as required.

GREEN THUMB GUIDE

Containers
Plant zinnias in tubs, pots and urns with a minimum depth of 6 to 8 inches. Dwarf varieties are best for window boxes; taller plants may need some support.

Position
A sunny location is best. Zinnias will grow in shade but produce fewer flowers. Because of their fragile stems zinnias should be sheltered from wind and heavy rain.

Soil
Use a standard potting mix.

Watering
Zinnias will tolerate periods of drought but normally prefer regular watering. Allow the soil to dry out slightly between waterings.

Feeding
Apply water-soluble fertilizer every two weeks.

General care
Deadhead regularly to prolong the flowering time and pinch out growing tips to encourage a branching, bushy shape.

Trees and shrubs

A wide variety of small trees and shrubs look and grow well in containers. Evergreens will make a year-round contribution to the terrace setting, while deciduous subjects will be appreciated at different seasons, perhaps for the beauty of their blossom or fruit, or for their foliage in fall.

Always buy from a reputable nursery or garden center. Before investing, discuss each subject's suitability for the situation you have in mind. Check on the plant's preferences for light and shelter, on its growing habit (vertical or spreading) and its eventual size.

Most small trees and shrubs will do well in standard soil, except those with marked preferences for acid or alkaline soils. Containers must always be well drained and of an appropriate size to allow for growth.

All trees and shrubs will benefit from an annual top dressing of fresh soil. Smaller, slow-growing shrubs may need an additional liquid feed in the summer months.

Each year, repot fast-growing shrubs and trees into larger containers. When they have reached the desired maximum height, you can take them out for an annual inspection (when unhealthy or damaged roots can be removed) and then return them to the same container.

Slow-growing flowering shrubs (such as camellias and azaleas) require little attention other than the removal of faded flowers and seed pods, and regular tidying and thinning.

JAPANESE MAPLE (Zone 5)
Acer palmatum
This deciduous bushy shrub or tree will grow slowly to a height of about 10 feet in a container, with a spread of up to 6 feet. Many varieties are available, their five-lobed leaves, ranging in color from pale-green through crimson or bronze. In some, the foliage is red in spring, bright green in summer and scarlet, yellow or orange in fall. The slender red or green branches make an attractive pattern even when bare of leaves.

Though it will tolerate a sunny position, the Japanese maple does best in filtered shade. Protect it from hot dry winds. Water regularly in warm weather. It prefers a lime-free soil, so in chalk or limestone regions, use rainwater or distilled water if possible. Feed monthly during the growing season.

STAGHORN SUMAC (Zone 3)
Rhus typhina
In a container, this easy-to-grow shrub or small tree will reach a height of some 10 feet with a spread of 12 feet. Its large leaves produce a "tropical" effect. Dark green on the surface and grayish underneath, they are covered in velvety brown hairs and turn bright orange or red in fall.

In fall the sumac bears attractive clusters of crimson fruit. These remain on the tree for most of the winter, gradually turning brown in color.

Japanese maple

Staghorn sumac

English yew

The staghorn sumac will grow in most standard soils, but dislikes a heavy alkaline content. It can withstand extremes of temperature, but prefers a sunny sheltered position.

ENGLISH YEW (Zone 6)
Taxus baccata
This slow-growing, long-lived evergreen conifer is bushy and erect, with broad, deep-green, needle-shaped leaves. It makes a good foil to containers planted with colorful flowers.

Container-grown yew trees will reach about 10 feet with a spread of 5 feet. Essentially a shade-lover, it will tolerate moderate sun but not direct hot sun. It also dislikes low temperatures and dry winds. In cold northern zones, it must be afforded the shelter of a garage or wall during winter.

This yew will thrive in standard soil. It should be watered regularly in hot weather and established specimens should be fed once a month from spring to fall. A word of warning: the bright-red fruit of the yew and its foliage are both poisonous if eaten.

JAPANESE QUINCE (Zone 4)
Chaenomeles japonica
This deciduous shrub will make a year-round contribution to its setting. The spread of its branches, particularly when trained against a wall, gives an "oriental" appearance. Its oriental quality is enhanced by the waxy, orange-scarlet flowers which contrast with the glossy rounded leaves.

Quince will grow to between 3 and 8 feet tall in a container, with a spread of 5 to 8 feet. Judicious pruning when the plant is in bud or in flower encourages healthy growth.

Plant quince in a standard soil and, in most zones, a position in full sun, though it does not like extremes of temperature. Water regularly in summer and, if necessary, protect it from winter cold by taking it into a garage or basement.

MEXICAN ORANGE (Zone 7)
Choisya ternata
A fast-growing evergreen shrub, Mexican orange produces a dense growth of yellow-green leaves which fan out in groups of three. In early summer, there are large clusters of fragrant white blossom.

Given a sunny sheltered spot, the Mexican orange will grow to a height and spread of 6 feet in a container. In the warmest zones, it will need protection from the hot summer sun. Similarly, in temperate and northern zones, protect it against frost and winter winds.

This plant does not like very alkaline soil. It should be planted in a special azalea potting mix. In chalk or limestone areas, rain or distilled water is best. Ensure that the container is well drained.

ROSE OF SHARON (Zone 5)
Hibiscus syriacus
A good subject for an informal setting, this deciduous shrub produces pink, purple or red flowers from mid-summer through fall in warmer zones. Varieties with single blooms are generally more attractive than doubles. 'Woodbridge,' illustrated below, has five rose-pink petals, each with a carmine eye. Bigger flowers are obtained by rigorous pruning in winter, cutting back the previous season's growth to two buds.

This hibiscus will grow to about 8 feet in a container, adopting a more spreading habit as it ages. Position in sun or partial shade. It will need winter protection in northern zones, particularly during its first two years. Water freely in warm weather and feed monthly during the active growth season.

MINIATURE ROSES (Zone 4)
Rosa sp.
New varieties of miniature rose are constantly appearing. Between 6 and 12 inches in height, they are ideal subjects for window boxes and smaller tubs on balconies or terraces. They are generally hardier than the hybrid tea roses, but their shallow root system means that they demand frequent watering, feeding and mulching. They should be pruned back to half their height in spring, after the risk of hard frosts is past.

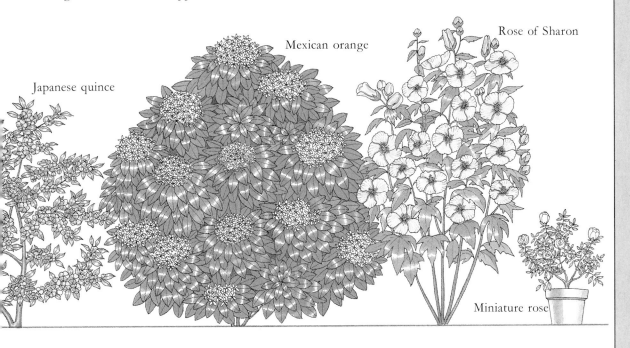

Japanese quince

Mexican orange

Rose of Sharon

Miniature rose

Climbing plants

Climbing plants may be used to enhance, disguise or conceal architectural features, or as a decorative focus in their own right. Plant imaginatively, for example cover old tree trunks with clematis or tumble Virginia creeper over balcony railings. Some, such as ivies and climbing hydrangeas, will cling without supports. Others – the twiners and twisters – will need canes, wires, strings or trellises to climb up. All supports should be durable, appropriate for their site and, for large woody climbers, strong, high and wide enough to accommodate the plant's spread.

Clematis

Passion flower

Chilean gloryflower

SHADY AREAS

IVY (Zone 5)
Hedera sp.
Best planted in full or semi-shade, ivies will tolerate full sun in temperate but not hot zones. Many species and varieties are available.

These evergreen woody vines cling with aerial roots. Water ivies freely in warm weather and feed once a month for vigorous growth. Height: 10 to 20 feet. Spread: to 12 feet.

CLIMBING HYDRANGEA (Zone 4)
Hydrangea anomala petiolaris
This deciduous clinging vine has attractive glossy leaves. Young stems are golden-brown; ivory-colored lacecap flowers come in summer. This climber will thrive in sunny places but does equally well in constantly shaded spots. Height: to 20 feet. Spread: 12 feet.

VIRGINIA CREEPER (Zone 3)
Parthenocissus quinquefolia
Prized for the beautiful foliage color in fall, this deciduous vine clings with sucker disks and is difficult to remove. It will thrive in semi-shade and needs feeding monthly through spring to fall. Water freely in warm weather.

SEMI-SHADED AREAS

HONEYSUCKLE (Zone 5)
Lonicera sp.
Depending on the species, you can get a vigorous twining evergreen or a deciduous shrub. Many species have heavily scented tubular flowers, in white, yellow or red, but the most fragrant types are often less showy. Choose *L. japonica* for scent and *L. sempervirens* for display.

Honeysuckles grow best in semi-shade, with their roots kept shaded and moist. Height: to 20 feet. Spread: to 15 feet.

WHITE JASMINE (Zone 7)
Jasminum officinale
A semi-evergreen to deciduous twiner, this jasmine has small, fragrant, trumpetlike flowers in summer. Water freely and feed monthly. If necessary, cut it back in winter to keep it tidy. Height: to 15 feet. Spread: to 5 feet.

CANARY NASTURTIUM (Zone 7)
Tropaeolum peregrinum
This vigorous climber has yellow frilled flowers and gray-green foliage. It is tolerant to semi-shade and full sun. Height: to 10 feet. Spread: to 15 feet.

SUNNY AREAS

CLEMATIS (Zone 5)
Clematis sp.
A great variety of species and cultivars are available of this deciduous climber. Clematis should be regularly fed and watered during the flowering period and the roots kept cool by screening the container. Clematis looks wonderful intertwined with another climber, such as wisteria, roses or pyracantha. Height: to 20 feet. Spread: 10 feet or more.

PASSION FLOWER (Zone 7)
Passiflora caerulea
A rampant deciduous climber, passion flower blooms all summer and into the fall. During this long flowering season, water freely and feed once every two weeks. Height: to 8 feet. Spread: 15 feet.

CHILEAN GLORYFLOWER (Zone 9)
Eccremocarpus scaber
In warmer zones, this vigorous tendril climber can be treated as a perennial; in northern zones, it is best sown as an annual. Beautiful orange, red or yellow tubular flowers bloom through summer into fall. Position in full sun. Height: to 8 feet. Spread: 3 feet.

Water gardens

Water has a most soothing effect in a garden and the plants that grow in or near a pond are beautiful and graceful, often with stunning flowers. A pond's wildlife is also fascinating. Fish, snails, insects and their larvae, water fleas and beetles, birds – there is interest all year round.

With the right combination of plants and animals, a miniature ecosystem soon becomes established and starts to look after itself. A note of caution – water, no matter how shallow, has its dangers, so always keep a close eye on children and pets playing near the pond.

It is surprisingly easy to create a water garden. Any large watertight container, with a minimum depth of 12 inches, is suitable (but 18 inches if you want fish in it). Thus, a reconstituted stone trough or an old sink can be used, or a wooden half-barrel made waterproof with a plastic lining, secured around the rim with rubber solution.

To make a "proper" pool you can excavate a hole and line it with plastic sheeting or you can sink a fiberglass bath in the ground, in both cases disguising the edges with rocks or paving. Site your water garden in a sunny area and not under a deciduous tree whose leaves will decay and foul the water in the long winter months.

Types of water plants
There are two main categories. The first consists of aquatic plants that live either completely submerged or floating on the surface. Canadian pondweed (*Anacharis*) and parrotfeather or water milfoil

(*Myriophyllum*) grow mainly as submerged aquatics and are excellent oxygenators. Such plants are absolutely vital to the health of the pond for they aerate the water and help to keep everything else alive.

Water lilies (*Nymphaea*) are the best known floating aquatics and come in white, pink, red and yellow varieties, with the most beautiful star-shaped flowers. Although rooted on the bottom of the pond, their leaves rise to the surface and spread out. There are other aquatics that are free-floating, such as water hyacinth (*Eichhornia*), with lilac flowers spotted with gold, and fairy moss or fern (*Azolla*), which forms a red carpet on the surface. The roots of these floating aquatics simply hang down into the water and do not need to be anchored in soil.

The second category are the marginal water plants. They like the wet boggy conditions in and around a pond and live happily on a shallow shelf at the edge of a

pond, with several inches of water covering their roots. Examples of marginal water plants include water arum (*Calla palustris*) with its heart-shaped leaves and white flowers; yellow marsh marigold (*Caltha palustris*); flowering rush (*Butomus umbellatus*) covered in pink heads in mid-summer; blue-flowering water mint (*Mentha aquatica*) with lemon-scented leaves; the clematislike flowers of bog iris (*Iris kaempferi*); and tiny sky-blue water forget-me-nots (*Myosotis palustris*).

Planting water plants
Fill your plastic planting basket with a good soil-based potting mix, having lined it with burlap or a fine nylon mesh to prevent the soil washing away. Ensure the soil is damp, with no air bubbles remaining, before planting. Then cover the surface with coarse gravel to keep the soil in place. Oxygenators can be planted in soil at the bottom of the pool.

PLANTING SCHEME

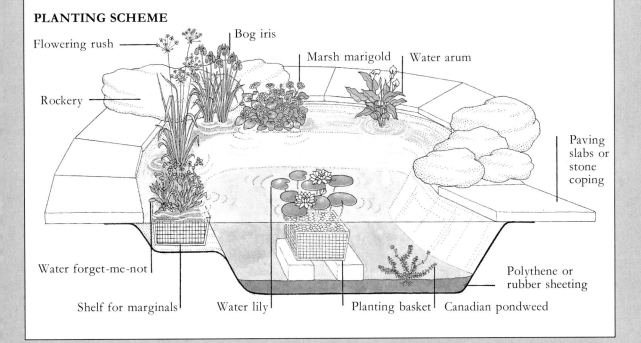

Flowering rush — Bog iris — Marsh marigold | Water arum

Rockery

Paving slabs or stone coping

Water forget-me-not

Polythene or rubber sheeting

Shelf for marginals | Water lily | Planting basket | Canadian pondweed

Herbs, vegetables and fruit

Window box and terrace gardeners can never hope to be self-sufficient in fruit and vegetables, but space limitations need not deprive them of the satisfaction of rearing some of their own produce. Many city gardeners have learned to be resourceful and imaginative in their exploitation of small spaces, making them incredibly productive.

With the recent widespread upsurge in enthusiasm for "growing your own" has come a marked change in our visual perception of many edible plants. Flowerbeds fringed with tender frilly green lettuces, cascades of wild strawberries in hanging baskets, tubs of fragrant rosemary, scarlet-flowering climbing beans with their handsome green foliage offset by a white wall – all provide aesthetic as well as gastronomic delight.

Here are some suggestions for herbs, vegetables and fruit that can easily be grown in containers. Space does not allow a detailed consideration of their individual cultivation or maintenance needs, nor exhaustive listings of species and cultivars. The aim is simply to suggest new directions.

HERBS
Culinary herbs grown in window boxes or on balconies should be the low-growing kind, since taller plants, such as dill and fennel, will not withstand buffeting by wind.

Quick-growing parsley, sweet marjoram, chives, coriander and chervil are good choices. If you use a lot of herbs in cooking, sow continuously for a constant supply. Grow mint in a separate container since it is so invasive.

Certain evergreen culinary herbs are prized for their decorative leaves and, often, their fragrance. These include rosemary, thyme and sage. Give these enough room to develop to a reasonable size and shape before you start harvesting.

Large half-barrels planted with standard bay trees are attractive and a pair of these trees flanking a terrace door or steps looks elegant.

Containers
Herb containers range from specially designed terracotta pots, with soil pockets at varying heights, to large tubs or troughs. All containers should be well drained and crocked.

A HARVEST FROM YOUR YARD

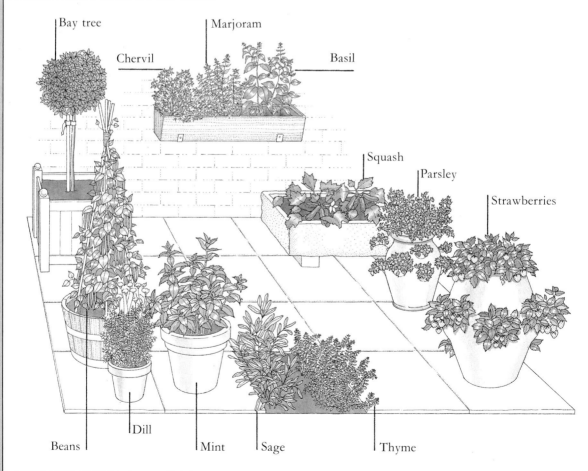

Bay tree · Marjoram · Chervil · Basil · Squash · Parsley · Strawberries · Beans · Dill · Mint · Sage · Thyme

Position and care

Most herbs like a sheltered sunny position, though some will tolerate semi-shade, and many prefer dry soil. Never water when the sun is shining on them and always use tepid water.

Here, in brief, are details of the approximate height (H) and spread (S) in containers, the preferred position (P), watering needs (W), propagation (Pr) and uses (U) of some common culinary herbs. They will all grow quite happily in a standard potting mix.

BASIL (Ocimum basilicum)

Annual. H: 2ft. S: 12in. P: Sheltered, sunny. W: Regularly in dry weather. Pr: Seed in spring. U: Good with pasta dishes, tomatoes, eggplant, zuccini, seafood.

CHERVIL (Anthriscus cerefolium)

Annual. H: 12in. S: 9in. P: Semi-shade. W: Likes water. Pr: Seed in spring or fall. U: Salads, soups, fish dishes, mornays.

CHIVES (Allium schoenoprasum)

Perennial. H: 10in. S: 8in. P: Semi-shade. W: Water liberally. Pr: Seed in spring. Division in spring or fall. U: Garnish for savory dishes.
Note: The more you pick, the better they grow. Deadhead to prevent early dying back.

MARJORAM, SWEET (Origanum majorana)

Perennial or half-hardy annual. H: 8in. S: 12in. P: Sunny, sheltered. W: Will tolerate dry soil. Water occasionally. Pr: Seed in spring or fall. Division in spring. U: In pasta and rice dishes, moussaka, pizzas, meatloaf, pork.

PARSLEY (Petroselinum crispum)

Perennial, usually grown as biennial or annual. H: 9in. S: 9in. W: Plentifully. Pr: Seed in spring. U: Flavoring and garnish.

ROSEMARY (Rosmarinus officinalis)

Evergreen shrub. H: 5ft. S: 5ft. P: Full sun. Grows well alongside sage. W: Will tolerate dryness. Pr: Seed in spring. Heel cuttings in spring. U: With lamb, zuccini, eggplant, lima beans.

SAGE (Salvia officinalis)

Evergreen shrub. H: 2ft. S: 1ft. P: Sunny, sheltered. Good companion plant for rosemary. W: Moderately. Pr: Seed in spring. Division or cuttings in spring or fall. U: Fish, duck, cheese, pork, beans.
Note: Plants should be cut back hard once they have flowered.

THYME (Thymus vulgaris)

Perennial. H: 10in. S: 12in. P: Sunny. W: Occasionally. Pr: Seed or cuttings, division or layering in spring or fall. U: With parsley, marjoram and bayleaf for traditional *bouquet garni*. Meat and vegetables.

VEGETABLES AND FRUIT

Dwarf varieties of tomatoes and beans have been specially developed for window boxes and other small containers. Normal-size plants may be grown in large individual pots or grouped in twos or threes in growing bags or other large containers. If you have room between plants or at the edges, use it for growing small herbs or an additional crop of lettuce. Climbing beans can be trained up trellises or tripods to add yet another visual dimension to your "vegescape."

Containers should be sited in a sunny sheltered spot. As with all containers, drainage is important. Use a standard potting mix or a soilless mix. Water and feed as indicated for the subject.

Usually, unless you require a large number of plants, it is better to buy plantlets rather than sow seed. Here are brief cultivation details for some of the more popular container vegetables.

EGGPLANTS

Plant one per large pot or two to a growing bag, as soon as risk of frost is over. Provide freestanding plastic-covered wire supports for growing bags, wooden stakes for individual pots.

Pinch out the growing tips when plants are 10 inches tall. Space out and secure branches to support. When four or five fruits have formed on each plant, pinch out all remaining flowers.

Keep soil moist. Feed regularly with standard plant food once fruits have reached the size of golfballs.

ZUCCINI

Set two plantlets to a growing bag in later spring. No support is necessary.

Keep soil moist but do not saturate. Feed with standard plant food once fruits are being harvested. Zuccini are best picked at between 4 and 6 inches long.
Note: Fruits should set without intervention. Withering larger female flowers are an indication that there are not enough pollinating insects around and the plant will need your help to set fruit.

CLIMBING BEANS

Grow from seed, sown as soon as all risk of frost is over. Provide support and help the small plants to find it, gently twisting the growing tips around wires or canes.

Keep soil moist but not saturated. Start feeding regularly once picking begins. Pick pods before bean seeds are visible inside them.

TOMATOES

When there is no danger of further frost, set one plant per large pot or three per growing bag. Provide stakes or supports for the plants.

Remove side shoots that appear at points where leaves join stems. When four or five trusses have formed, nip out the growing tips, leaving two leaves above the top truss. This "stopping" is not necessary with bush varieties.

Keep soil moist but not saturated. Start feeding when the second truss is setting and stop when the top one has set and the fruits are beginning to swell.

STRAWBERRIES

These popular fruits will grow in specially designed terracotta or plastic pots or towers, in growing bags or any other large container. Set plants out in late summer or in spring. Eight or so will fit in a standard growing bag. Leave them overwinter in a sheltered spot where they will benefit from any sun available. In very cold zones, delay planting until late spring or early summer.

Water the soil when it seems to have dried out on the surface. Feed in spring. To maintain, remove dead leaves after harvesting and cut off any runners that are not needed. Pot these up to get fresh young plants next year.

Index of Scientific names

A
Acer palmatum 64
Agapanthus africanus 35
  – *albidus* 35
  – *variegatus* 35
Agave americana 36
  – *marginata* 36
Ageratum 12
  – *houstonianum* 41
Allium schoenoprasum 69
Amaranthus caudatus 37
Anacharis canadensis 67
Anthriscus cerefolium 69
Antirrhinum majus 42
Asparagus densiflorus 6
Azolla 67

B
Butomus umbellatus 24, 67

C
Calla palustris 67
Caltha palustris 67
Callistephus chinensis 43
Campanula poscharskyana 38
Chaenomeles japonica 65
Chamaecyparis 12
Clematis 66
Chlorophytum comosum 34
Choisya ternata 65
Chrysanthemum frutescens 22
  – × *spectabile* 41
Cobaea scandans 44–45

D
Dahlia × *cultorum* 46
Dimorphotheca sinuata 47
Dorotheanthus bellidiformis 41

E
Eccremocarpus scaber 66
Eichhornia 67
Erica carnea 12
Eschscholzia californica 48
Euonymus 6

H
Hedera 6, 66
  – *helix* 12
Hibiscus syriacus 65
Hydrangea anomala petiolaris 22, 66

I
Iberis umbellata 49
Ipomoea tricolor 50
Iris kaempferi 49

J
Jasminum officinale 66
Juniperus 12

L
Lantana camara 39
Lavatera trimestris 51
Lilium candidum 11
Lonicera 66
  – *japonica* 66
  – *sempervirens* 66

M
Mentha aquatica 67
Mimulus luteus 52
  – *ringens* 52
  – *variegatus* 52
Myosotis palustris 67
Myriophyllum 67

N
Nemesia strumosa 53
Nicotiana alata 54
Nymphaea 67

O
Ocimum basilicum 69
Origanum majorana 69

P
Parthenocissus quinquefolia 66
Passiflora caerulea 66
Pelargonium × *hortorum* 55
  – *peltatum* 13
Penstemon × *gloxinioides* 56
  – *hartwegii* 56
Petroselinum crispum 69
Petunia × *hybrida* 57
Phacelia campanularia 58

R
Rhus typhina 64–65
Rosa 65
Rosmarinus officinalis 69

S
Salvia 59
  – *farinacea* 59
  – *officinalis* 69
  – *patens* 59
  – *splendens* 59
Schizanthus 60
  – *grahami* 60
  – *pinnatus* 60
  – × *wisetonensis* 60
Senecio 12, 61
  – *cineraria* 61
Solanum pseudocapsicum 6

T
Taxus baccata 65
Thunbergia alata 62
Thymus vulgaris 69
Tropaeolum majus 41
  – *peregrinum* 66

Z
Zinnia elegans 63

FAMILIES
Acanthaceae 62
Agavaceae 36
Amaranthaceae 37

Campanulaceae 38
Compositae 61, 63
Convolvulaceae 50
Cruciferae 49

Labiatae 59
Liliaceae 35

Malvaceae 51

Papaveraceae 48
Polemoniaceae 44

Scrophulariaceae 42, 52, 53, 56
Solonaceae 60

Verbanaceae 39

Index of Common names

A
African blue lily (agapanthus) 34, 35
Agave 34, 36
Aloe 34
Alpine plants 24, 30
Alpine strawberry 24
Annuals 40–63
Asparagus fern 6
Aubretia 24
Azalea 29, 64

B
Basil 69
Beans, climbing 69
Begonia 9, 24, 25
Bellflower 38
Black-eyed Susan 62
Bog iris 67
Bulbs 11, 12
Busy lizzy 5, 9, 28
Butterfly flower 60

C
Cacti 11, 30, 34
California poppy 48
Camellia 64
Campanula 24, 38
Canadian pondweed 67
Candytuft 49
Cathedral bell 44–45
Ceanothus 25
Chamaecyparis 12, 25
Chervil 69
Chives 69
Chrysanthemum 22, 26, 41
Chilean gloryflower 66
China aster 43
Clematis 22, 25, 66
Climbing hydrangea 22, 66
Conifers, dwarf 7, 12, 25
Crassula 34
Cup-and saucer vine, *see* Cathedral bell

D
Dahlia, dwarf 46
Dusty miller 12, 61

E
Eggplant 69
English yew 65

F
Fairy moss/fern 67
Flowering rush 24, 67
Flowering tobacco 54

G
Gardenia 5
Geranium 6, 9, 13, 24, 26, 31, 55
Grape vine 22, 25
Grasses 24, 25

H
Harebell phacelia 58
Heather 12, 29
Herb tree-mallow 51
Herbs 25, 68–69
Hollyhock 51
Honeysuckle 22, 25, 30, 66

I
Iris, beardless 25
Ivy 6, 12, 22, 66

J
Japanese maple 64
Japanese quince 65
Jasmine 27, 66
Jerusalem cherry 6
Juniper 25

L
Lantana 39
Livingstone daisy 24, 41
Lobelia 9, 13
Love-lies-bleeding 37

M
Maple tree 24
Marguerite 24
Marigold, Cape 47
Marjoram, sweet 69
Marsh marigold 25, 67
Mexican orange 65
Monkey flower 52
Morning glory 50

N
Nasturtium 41, 66
Nemesia 53
Nerine lily 11

P
Parrotfeather 67
Parsley 69
Passion flower 30, 34, 66
Pelargonium, *see* Geranium
Penstemon 56
Petunia 9, 20, 57
Poor man's orchid, *see* Butterfly flower

R
Rhododendron 29
Rock plants 32
Rose of Sharon 65
Rosemary 69
Roses, miniature 25, 65

S
Sage 59, 69
Snapdragon 42, 52, 56
Spider plant 34
Staghorn sumac 64–65
Strawberries 69
Succulents 34

T
Tassel flower, *see* Love-lies-bleeding
Thyme 69
Tomatoes 19, 69

V
Vegetables 19, 68–69
Verbena 27
Virginia creeper 22, 66

W
Wallflower 12
Water arum 67
Water forget-me-not 67
Water hyacinth 67
Water lily 24, 67
Water milfoil, *see* Parrotfeather
Water plants 24, 25, 67
Water mint 67
Wild flowers 24

Y
Yucca 34

Z
Zinnia 63
Zonal pelargonium, *see* Geranium
Zuccini 69

Acknowledgments

Publisher	**Bruce Marshall**	Contributors	**Don Binney** **Carole Devaney**
Creative Director	**John Bigg**	Text Editing	**Jinny Johnson**
Editor	**Anne Kilborn**	Picture Coordinator	**Zilda Tandy**
Managing Editor	**Ruth Binney**	Production Coordination	**Barry Baker** **Janice Storr**
Art Editor	**Pauline Faulks**		

Torstar Books Inc.
41 Madison Avenue
Suite 2900
New York, NY 10010

Marshall Editions, an editorial group that specializes in the design and publication of practical and scientific subjects for the general reader, prepared this book in collaboration with ICA-förlaget AB, Sweden. Marshall has written and illustrated standard works on gardening, cookery, needlecraft, photography, biology and technology which are recommended for schools and libraries, as well as for popular reference.

Series Consultant

Maggie Oster is advisor to *The Complete Gardening Guide* and has written extensively on the subjects of plants and gardens. She was a major contributor to the *Time-Life Encyclopedia of Gardening* and from 1982–83 was producer and presenter of the monthly television show "Maggie's Garden" on WLKY-TV.

Photographs

Cover photograph Spike Powell
Photograph pp. 2–3 Spike Powell
All other photography courtesy
ICA-förlaget AB

Artwork

p. 4 Dennis Hawkins
pp. 8, 10, 12, 14, 16, 18, 19, 24, 25, 33, 35, 44, 52
Norman Bancroft-Hunt
pp. 64–68 Karen Daws/John Craddock
Endpapers Hayward and Martin

Plants and containers

Plants: cover, pp. 2–3 Longmans Ltd; containers: Patio and Rassell.